Reap the Whirlwind

By Susan E. Hilliard

Illustrated by Ned O.

 STANDARD PUBLISHING
Cincinnati, Ohio   24-03987

Library of Congress Cataloging-in-Publication Data

Hilliard, Susan E.
  Reap the whirlwind / by Susan E. Hilliard.
    p. cm.
  Summary: The reader makes choices about dramatic events in the lives of Deborah, Samson, and Gideon while visiting them to find out why God appointed them to judge Israel.
  ISBN 0-87403-727-1
  1. Deborah (Biblical judge)—Juvenile literature. 2. Sampson Biblical judge)—Juvenile leterature. 3. Gideon (Biblical judge)—Juvenile literature. 4. Plot-your-own stories. [1. Deborah (Biblical judge) 2. Samson (Biblical judge) 3. Gideon (Biblical judge) 4. Bible stories—O.T. 5. Plot-your-own stories.]
  I. Title.
  BS579.J83H54 1990
  222'.320922—dc20   90-33559
                                                                    CIP
                                                                    AC

Edited by Theresa C. Hayes

Attention, Reader!

You cannot read this book as you would any other. You are embarking upon a very special quest for answers to questions you will soon receive. On your quest you will travel in a chariot of fire and you will sometimes be allowed to choose between alternative events and times. When you decide, the chariot will take you swiftly to the destination of your choice.

When you find your chariot, be sure to look for two scrolls of parchment in it. The first is a vital archive of facts that can aid you in making the right choices. The second scroll will contain the object of your quest.

Also in the chariot, you will find rules for your travel and appropriate clothing.

And now, begin the adventure!

The Chariot

A chariot of fire stands before you. The chariot itself seems solid enough, although it appears to be completely engulfed in flames. Your heart thudding, you step closer and notice that the fire is not hot—only pleasantly warm. Through the shimmering flames you see a beautiful horse hitched to the chariot, standing patiently. The beast seems so serene that you find your heart is not hammering quite so violently, and you hesitantly step into the chariot. Nothing happens. You are surrounded by flames, yet nothing is burning. You step farther into the chariot, and notice a plain wooden box on the floor. Upon the box is written "Rules for Travel." You open the box.

On the inside of the lid, you read . . . .

Rules For Travel

You must follow these rules on your journey. If you do not, the chariot will return you to the present, and you will never be able to complete your quest.

I. You may not change history in any way — you are only an observer.
II. You may choose only from the alternatives that you are given.
III. You may not bring twentieth-century customs, clothing, or equipment with you. Tell no one you may meet of your journey.
IV. You may not bring any souvenirs of your journey home with you.

You will find that language differences will not be a problem for you — you will automatically think and speak in the language of your host place and time.

Inside the box you see folds of tan cloth, and an almost-hidden, yellowed parchment. You pull out the cloth and grab the parchment as it begins to float to the ground. A quick glance shows you a crude sketch of a man in a short-sleeved tunic which is girded at the waist and falls to the ankles. Holding the tunic in front of you, you decide that it just might fit.

You quickly remove your twentieth-century clothing and pull the tunic over your head. A sash nestles in the box, and you tie it securely around your waist. Finally you pull on the leather sandals — the very last item in the wooden box. You scoop up your discarded clothes, wad them into a ball, and hurl them into a nearby bush.

The beautiful horse begins pawing the ground impatiently, and you drop to your knees inside the chariot to search for your instructions. In the dark forward corners, your groping fingers find something that feels like a cylinder of paper. You pull it out with trembling haste, and a smaller cylinder falls from inside the larger one.

You break the seal on the smaller scroll and unroll it to read . . . .

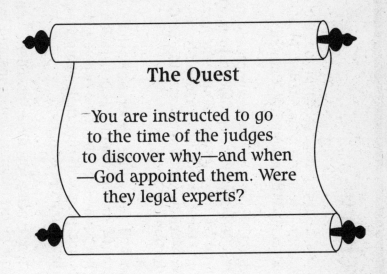

The Quest

You are instructed to go
to the time of the judges
to discover why—and when
—God appointed them. Were
they legal experts?

You remember vaguely that there were more
than a few judges, and wonder why there were
so many. The thought stirs in your brain that
Samson was a judge—and you decide that this is
going to be pretty interesting!

Swiftly you unroll the larger scroll and glance
through it. Although it looks like facts to study
for a history exam, you decide that you had better pay close attention to the information. Carefully, you read . . . .

Archives

I. After Moses led the Hebrews from captivity in Egypt to the border of the promised land, he died and was buried by God. Joshua was then appointed to lead the people into Canaan.

II. When the Hebrews settled in Canaan, they were completely surrounded by pagan cultures. Hebrews were forbidden to marry pagans, since intermingling of the cultures would encourage the Hebrews to worship false idols. Unfortunately most Hebrews did not heed the warning, and soon worship of God was in danger of total extinction.

III. After the death of Joshua and the entire generation who had experienced God's deliverance in the exodus, a generation of Israelites arose who did not know the Lord. The twelve tribes, which had been united as one people during their wanderings, went their separate ways in the land of Canaan.

IV. The Midianites were a fierce tribe of desert-dwellers, who oppressed the tribe of Judah by destroying their crops and livestock. They rode swift camels, and were greatly feared.

V. The Canaanites, a sophisticated people, were completely controlled by pagan fertility cults. They worshiped nature with cruel and inhuman sacrifices.

VI. The Philistines, powerful and warlike sea people, were mortal enemies of Israel.

VII. The Ammonites were descendants of Abraham's nephew, Lot. Their national god was Molech, whom they honored by the sacrifice of children—burned alive at Molech's altars.

VIII. Mesopotamia was known as the land between two rivers—the Tigris and Euphrates—also known as Babylon. Among the gods honored here were Ishtar, Dagon, and numerous others.

IX. The Moabites, known as "the people of Chemosh", worshipped their god Chemosh by burning children in sacrifice. Their kingdom was well-organized and their buildings splendid, but their worship was horrible and cruel.

X. The first judge appointed by God was Othniel, and the last was Samson. There were twelve in all, covering the period from Joshua's death until the anointing of Saul as king over Israel.

You turn
the parchment
over and are
relieved to see a
roughly-drawn
map. *Wow! The
Hebrews really
were surrounded,*
you realize as
you study the
map. Then
you reroll the
parchment and
tuck it firmly
into your sash;
you have a
strong feeling
that you will
need to refer to
it again—
you'll never
keep all these
names straight
without some help!

You pick up the cool leather reins, excitement racing like a current through your body. The steed's nostrils flare and its hooves paw the ground impatiently. Almost breathless, you pull the reins taut, and suddenly. . . .

(At the Beginning)

You find yourself on the summit of a low hill. Dusk paints the western sky gold and pink and the hills around you a soft purple. The sound of a strangled sob makes you whirl around to confront the mutinous face of a girl about your age.

You look at her tear-stained face in sympathy. "What's the matter?" you ask quietly. "Why are you crying?"

Her jaw juts fiercely as she growls huskily, "I'm *not* crying." She wipes the tears off her cheeks with a ruthless swipe of one tanned hand and glares at you.

Nervously, you shift from one foot to the other — *this adventure is not off to a very promising start*, you reflect. You are wondering what you should say next when the girl suddenly sinks to her knees and her face crumples in grief.

"Oh, Joshua . . . !" she sobs, "Why did you have to die? Who will lead us now?"

"Joshua?" you question softly. "Do you mean the Joshua who led your people after Moses died?"

"Of course!" she explodes. "Why do you ask such a question? Are you a stranger?"

"Yes," you reply honestly.

"Oh!" she gasps. "I'm sorry I was so rude! Joshua would not want me to be so. I wish I could offer you the hospitality of shelter and food, but . . . " she struggles with tears again and continues bravely, "I don't know what I'm going to do, with Joshua gone."

You stare at her blankly, wondering why she should be so upset at the death of the Hebrew leader.

"He took care of my little brother and me, you see," she explains forlornly. "We are orphans, and Joshua took us into his tent. He was the head of the tribe of Ephraim," she adds proudly.

Horrified at her plight, you stammer, "But surely *someone* will take care of you and your brother, now that Joshua is dead!"

She nods sadly. "Oh yes, I don't think we'll starve. But I am frightened for my people!"

"Frightened?" you echo, looking at the soft purple hills around you. "What are you afraid of?"

The girl's eyes grow wide. "We are living in the midst of a land filled with idol worship!" she breathes. "The angel of the Lord *told* us not to make any covenants with the inhabitants of this land—and we were supposed to tear down their altars to pagan gods. But we have not obeyed," her voice sinks to a terrified whisper. "The Lord said that He would no longer drive the people out before us, and that their gods would be a snare to us. With Joshua gone . . . who will serve the Lord? Who will remember Him?"

"Wait a minute!" you protest. "Just because a great leader is gone doesn't mean that everyone will forget the Lord who brought you out of captivity in Egypt!"

The girl smiles wanly. "You would be surprised how quickly people forget," she answers sadly. "Even after God sent the ten plagues to Egypt, delivered our people from slavery, and parted the Red Sea, the people were grumbling within two months, and made a golden idol to worship instead of the Lord God!"

That's true, you think to yourself. *It is hard to believe how quickly they forgot about the awesome things God had done!"*

"Do you see why I fear for my people?" the girl continues.

You nod miserably. "But surely everyone has learned the lesson since then," you protest feebly.

A silvery crescent of moon peeps over the distant hills and stars sparkle into life in the black-velvet sky as the girl sighs. "Well," she says slowly, "I will never forget the very last words Joshua spoke." Her dark eyes are luminous with unshed tears. "He said, 'As for me and my house, we will serve the

Lord.' And that is what *I* will do all *my* life long!" she says firmly. "I will not forget the Lord God of Israel!" She squares her shoulders and walks slowly down the hill.

Bright flames suddenly dance all around you, and you find yourself standing in the chariot of fire. Still amazed at the flames that warm but do not burn, you are suddenly startled by the sound of a low musical voice throbbing in the silence.

"It is time now for your first decision," chimes the voice. You look searchingly at the beautiful, milky-white steed, for the voice seems to come from there—although you cannot be certain.

"You will go forward in time now, to a generation who does not know the Lord. All of Joshua's generation has died. The sons of Israel have forgotten the Lord their God, and have been oppressed by the king of Mesopotamia. Here is your choice," continues the voice. "You may see the judge, Othniel, or you may see the king of Mesopotamia. Which will you choose?"

My quest is to find out why God appointed judges, you remind yourself as you take the smooth leather reins into your hands. After thinking carefully, you make your choice.

If you decide to see the judge Othniel, go to page 31.

If you decide to see the king of Mesopotamia, go to page 23.

(You Have Decided to Go Back in Time to Moses)

A massive, craggy mountain towers over you. In the level plain at its foot, tents cluster as far as you can see. Sunrise paints the landscape with a crimson and gold brush, and you hear the sleepy calls of birds just waking. A buzz of angry voices rises in the still dawn air, and you see crowds of men and woman picking their way through the tents. You turn at the sound of a tired sigh behind you.

A man stands on an outcropping of rock wearily surveying the approaching crowd. His broad shoulders are slumped in fatigue, and lines carve deep grooves on his intelligent face. He sighs again, then jumps easily to the ground and crosses in swift strides to a large tent.

"Good morning, Moses, my son-in-law!" calls a voice. A silver-haired man steps from the tent, his chest expanding as he drinks in the dew-drenched morning air.

Moses smiles with pleasure. "Good morning to you, Jethro. It is good to have you here in my tent."

The older man frowns suddenly, his piercing eyes fastened on Moses' face. "Yesterday I saw you sit from morning to evening, Moses. What is this thing that you are doing for the people? Why do you alone sit as judge and all the people stand about you from morning until evening?"

Moses sits heavily on the ground in front of his tent. "Because the people come to me to inquire of God," he answers soberly.

Jethro places a gnarled old hand fondly on his son-in-law's shoulder. "But Moses," he pleads, "you are weary."

Moses smiles up at the older man. "When the people have a dispute, they come to me," he says slowly, "and I judge between a man and his neighbor, and make known the statutes of God and His laws."

Squatting on the ground beside Moses, Jethro frowns. "The thing that you are doing is not good. You will surely wear out, both yourself and these people who are with you, for the task is too heavy for you; you cannot do it alone."

"I *must* do it, Jethro!" moans Moses. "How else are the disputes to be settled?"

The angry hum of voices is growing louder and you look up to see lines of quarreling men and women stretching as far as the eye can see. *How can he ever listen to all these people?* you wonder.

Jethro's arm encircles Moses' shoulders. "Now listen to me," he says firmly. "I shall give you counsel, and God be with you. You be the people's representative before God, and you bring the disputes to God. Then teach them the statutes and the laws, and make known to them the way in which they are to walk, and the work they are to do."

Moses listens to his father-in-law intently, a puzzled frown on his face. "Furthermore," continues Jethro briskly, "you shall select out of all the people able men who fear God, men of truth, those who hate dishonest gain; and you shall place these men over the rest, as leaders of thousands, of hundreds, of fifties and of tens."

A slow smile begins to dawn on Moses' face as Jethro goes on, "And let them judge the people at all times; and let it be that every major dispute they will bring to you, but every minor dispute they themselves will judge. So it will be easier for you, and they will bear the burden with you. If you do this thing and God so commands you, then you will be able to endure, and all these people also will go to their place in peace!"

Moses springs to his feet as if the weight of the world had just been removed from his back—and Jethro grins delightedly. *The first judges!* you think in excitement. *Moses himself appointed judges to settle disputes and to help the people walk in God's ways!*

Moses and Jethro disappear in the flames of the chariot of fire, as the voice sounds bell-like in your ear. "I take you forward now to see Joshua, Moses' successor. Mark well what you learn there."

Eagerly you take the reins in your hands.

Go to page 19.

(You Have Come to See Joshua, Moses' Successor)

Soft evening breezes fan your cheeks and the western sky is ablaze with shades of purple and gold. A multitude of people sit cross-legged on the hillside, looking up at an old man standing on the summit. A girl next to you smiles radiantly, and you recognize her from the very beginning of your adventure: she is the orphan girl whom Joshua took into his family.

"Isn't it grand?" she trills, pointing to the crowd of thousands. "All of Israel is here!"

A baby wails in the lap of a tired-looking woman seated almost at your feet and the girl expertly scoops the baby into her arms. The mother smiles gratefully, and the girl's eyes twinkle. "Sh-h-h, baby!" she whispers. "You must be quiet so we can hear what Joshua is going to say!" The baby crows with laughter as your companion makes an outrageous face. Silence spreads through the throng as the old man on the hill raises his hands for attention. Joshua's voice rings out, surprisingly strong and hearty.

"I am old, advanced in years," he begins, "and you have seen all that the Lord your God has done to all these nations because of you, for the Lord your God is He who has been fighting for you. Be very firm, then, to keep and do all that is written in the book of the law of Moses."

A strangled sob gurgles in the girl's throat as she watches Joshua with love shining in her eyes. "He is saying good-bye," she whispers.

"You are to cling to the Lord your God, as you have done to this day," Joshua's voice rings out triumphantly. "For the Lord has driven out great and strong nations from before you; and as for you, no man has stood before you to this day. One of your men puts to flight a thousand, for the Lord your God is He who fights for you, just as He promised you."

Even the trill of birds overhead is hushed as

Joshua continues. "Take diligent care to love the Lord your God. For if you ever go back and cling to the rest of these nations, and intermarry with

them, so that you associate with them and they with you . . . " the old man raises a warning fist, "know with certainty that the Lord your God will not continue to drive these nations out from before you; but they shall be a snare and a trap to you, and a whip on your sides and thorns in your eyes!" he thunders.

The hair on the back of your neck prickles as you realize that Israel will not only take pagan wives, but will actually worship idols—and you look long and hard at Joshua. You remember that he was born a slave in Egypt—that he shivered in his reed house when the Death Angel passed over the houses of the children of Israel to strike the first-born of Egypt dead. Joshua's warning is unmistakable—if Israel forgets the Lord, and worships idols, the surrounding nations will oppress her!

Joshua, and the thousands of people before him, disappear as the flames of the chariot surround you. Reluctantly you pick up the reins, for you know that you are almost at the end of your adventure. The gentle voice sounds, "Now you will go forward in time, little one. I take you now to the judge Jephthah."

Go to page 115.

(You Have Decided to See the King of Mesopotamia)

Shivering in the deep shadows of a huge marble column, you peer cautiously into the vast room. On a dais not far from where you are standing, a man slouches in an ornate wooden chair. Gems imbedded in the polished carving wink in the flickering torchlight. A heavy gold chain hangs around the man's neck, and a sun and moon—also fashioned from gold—dangle from the chain. Thick bracelets encircle his arms, and he watches from bored eyes as servants scurry to and fro across the room.

A soldier strides toward the dais and the king shifts in his chair, his eyes coming alive with interest. "Well, my captain?" purrs the king. "What tribute have you brought me from my Israelites?"

The soldier bows low, then straightens—his mouth a grim line. "Greetings, great Cushan-Rishathaim. You will not be pleased, I fear."

"And why is that?" snaps the king, his brows drawing together in a murderously angry frown.

The soldier shrugs. "They are a worthless people, my king. They have no exquisite ceramic as the Greeks do, they have no antiques from Egypt, they have little gold—even their fruits are not as varied and tasty as ours! A little grain, a few animals—that is the only tribute they can pay you, O King."

The king's dark eyes glitter furiously. "For eight years I have taken tribute from Israel. Are you telling me you have come back empty-handed?"

The soldier eyes the angry king calmly. "Not

empty-handed, sire. But eight years of oppression have dampened their spirits somewhat. Perhaps they are not quite as enthusiastic about what they provide to the king as they once were!"

Golden reflections from the king's jewelry dance crazily around the room as the king leaps to his feet. The chair crashes heavily to the ground, and he claps his hands sharply. "So the Israelites are no longer enthusiastic?" he roars. "We shall soon see about that!"

White-faced servants rush wide-eyed to the foot of the dais. Barely looking at them, the king commands, "Ready my chariot! And you!" he barks, pointing imperiously at the soldier, "Summon my men. I shall lead the army at first light tomorrow, and we shall teach the Israelites about *enthusiasm* with our swords at their throats!"

The king steps swiftly off the dais and strides straight toward you. Your heart thudding, you shrink back into the shadows, but his furious face is suddenly inches from your own. An iron grip fastens on your arm and the king's cruel eyes sparkle with malice. "Oh yes, dog," he hisses, "I have seen you cowering in the shadows! Perhaps I will allow *you* to insure my success," he grins wickedly. "Take this youngster to the priests," he orders over his shoulder to the soldier. "I desire him to have a special part in our military mission. The priests in the temple of Adad-Milki will know how the youngster may best serve the purpose!"

Wooden-faced, the soldier salutes his king and grips you firmly. He propels you forward through a doorway into a dark hall, lined with guttering

torches. Your mouth is dry with terror, for you have a terrible feeling about this—the king intended no good, you are certain.

You and your guard reach the end of the corridor and you blink in the light of day. The soldier looks down at you, his mouth twisted with disgust. "Be off with you," he growls softly. "And do not show your face in the palace again. I want no part in your being sacrificed to a bloodthirsty god! Go!" he hisses, pounding your back hard.

Sacrificed! You cannot believe how easily the king ordered your death, and you break into a blind run to get away from the palace. Suddenly the welcome flames of the chariot engulf you, and you sink gratefully against the side.

"You have seen the king of Aram," says the voice softly. "He oppressed the Israelites for eight years. You may now go to see the Moabites, another people who oppressed the Israelites. Or you may see a temple in Haran, which is a city in Mesopotamia. Which will you choose?"

Shuddering, you decide that neither choice sounds particularly appealing; but you take up the reins and make your decision.

If you decide to see the Moabites, go to page 36.

If you decide to see a temple in Haran, go to page 27.

(You Have Decided to See a Temple in Haran)

The moon paints your shadow across a flight of stone steps between two huge columns. Soft night breezes lift your hair gently, but wildly harsh laughter echoing from the building seems out of place in this soft, moonlit night. A man staggers drunkenly from the doorway between the pillars, followed by a woman. The woman's brightly-painted face looms crazily, her lips a gash of scarlet in her white face.

"May the goddess bring you good fortune!" the woman calls, her voice rising in a grating giggle.

The man grins crookedly as he lurches against the pillar. "She will, my sweet priestess," he replies. "Have I not worshiped her this very night?" He staggers down the steps, and your flesh crawls with revulsion as you look at him. A shriek erupts from the temple above, slicing through the silent night. You decide that you have seen enough of this temple in Haran—you do not wish to go inside!

"Here—you!" bellows the man as he catches sight of you. "Let me introduce you to the priestess of Ishtar!" He lunges toward you, but falls heavily on the ground. He reaches out and grabs your ankle with his sweaty hand. You jerk your foot out of his grasp and break into a run across the courtyard heading for an archway yawning black in the stone wall beyond. A glance over your shoulder reveals the man clambering awkwardly to his feet, shaking his fist angrily at you. You run even faster, for you are absolutely certain that you *do not* want to meet the priestess tonight—or any night!

Your chest heaving, you race through narrow streets that twist and turn haphazardly. At last you see the city gates, and you rush through—to come to a stop just outside. Your heart hammers and your mouth is dry as you stand on the level ground outside the city of Haran. Bee-hived-shaped stone houses stand silent and eerie beneath the white moon, their jet-black shadows sharp on the ground. Jackals call in the distance, their throbbing cries lonely in the night.

You slump against the stone wall still warm from the day, letting your heart and breath slow. *So this is how the people of Mesopotamia worship*, you reflect in disgust. You suspect that many people might be drawn to such a drunken, wicked pagan god—and you shiver. Remembering your archives scroll, you pull it hastily from your sash. You can read it easily in the bright moonlight.

Just as you thought—the goddess Ishtar was worshiped, as well as Dagon and many others. Perhaps even more evil existed here than that you have just encountered. You reroll the scroll and stuff it back in your sash—and almost shout for joy as the pure flames of the chariot of fire envelop you. However, a question burns inside you. "Surely the Israelites did not fall into worship of such wicked idols?" you ask.

The steed's voice floats gently in the bright moonlight. "Do you not know anyone who turns from God to worship pleasure and self?"

Uncomfortable, you realize that *many* are tempted to worship at those altars—and that perhaps people are not very different from age to age.

"Now for your decision," continues the voice gently. "I may take you to see the Canaanites, a people who oppressed the Israelites. Or you may choose to see the Moabites, who did the same. Which will you decide?"

Wondering which decision would help you more on your quest, you take the reins thoughtfully in hand and pull them taut.

If you decide to see the Canaanites,
go to page 59.

If you decide to see the Moabites,
go to page 36.

(You Have Decided
to See the Judge Othniel)

Darkness presses down upon you like a living presence, and strangled screams in the distance make you shiver. As you strain to see, the moon suddenly bursts from the clouds that were shielding it. Black shapes of trees spring into view, and you see that you are on a high hill in the midst of a thick grove of trees. As your eyes become more accustomed to the dimness, you see a woman straining to lift a heavy stone from a tall pile of rocks in a clearing.

You look furtively over your shoulder, but see no one else. Carefully, you walk toward the woman. "Here, let me help," you offer softly, but even the sound of your own voice in this eerie night makes you jump.

The woman turns, her face suspicious. She studies you for a moment, then seems to like what she reads in your face. "Thank you, young stranger," she replies with a tired sigh. "These rocks are heavier than I had thought!"

You lay your hands upon the topmost rock, hoisting it up. "What do you want me to do with it?" you ask, panting.

"Throw it down, my friend!" answers the woman sharply.

You hurl it away from you, your fingers slipping on the rock's sticky, moist surface. "What's on this rock, anyway?" you ask in disgust as you wipe your hands on your tunic.

"Blood!" comes the whispered reply. "The blood of innocents sacrificed to Asteroth!"

Violent shudders sweep over your frame, and you struggle with nausea. "Who sacrificed up here?" you whisper.

The woman's pale face sags with sorrow. "Israelites," she answers in a low voice. "Israelites who do not remember the Lord their God."

You stare it her, thunderstruck. She reaches for you suddenly, almost pulling you off balance. "Hush." she hisses urgently. "Someone is coming! We must hide quickly from the soldiers of the Mesopotamian king!"

She tugs you behind her toward the nearest tree, which has a twisted, thick trunk, overgrown with vines. You both sink down soundlessly into the thick undergrowth, watching the moonlit clearing with wide eyes.

A short, thickset man strides confidently into view, his drawn sword flashing dully in the pale light. He frowns fiercely at the pile of stones in the center of the clearing. "Pull this wicked altar down!" he roars, as several other soldiers jog into sight over the crest of the hill.

"Othniel!" your companion breathes. "We're safe! Othniel is here! The Spirit of the Lord has come upon Othniel!" She rises swiftly to her feet, pulling you up beside her, and crosses the clearing toward the man.

"Hannah!" he exclaims gladly as he sees the woman. "You have begun the work of tearing down the altar already! You were taking a terrible risk, you know." His homely face is lit by a radiant smile of infinite tenderness, and you find yourself drawn to this man of God.

Hannah smiles shyly. "I do not count the risk, Othniel," she replies. "For years, I have been tearing down these evil altars every time I find them! If I am put to death for it . . ." she shrugs carelessly. "I count that as gain. 'As for me and my house, we will serve the Lord,'" she finishes simply.

Electrified, you look sharply at the woman. Her dark, luminous eyes shine with love and faith from her middle-aged face. *Could this be the same girl who mourned the death of Joshua?* you wonder.

The Hebrew soldiers have finished tearing down the altar, and cluster around Othniel. "We have won, Othniel!" shouts the youngest proudly. "The soldiers of Mesopotamia will not trouble us again!"

Othniel's face becomes grave as he faces the young soldier. "*Why* did we win, Caleb?"

The young soldier flushes, and his gaze falls to the ground. "I wasn't being arrogant," he murmurs. "Well," he continues with a gleam of a smile, "maybe a little arrogant."

Othniel roars with good-natured laughter as the other soldiers join in. Sheepishly, the young soldier's gaze rests on Othniel's face. "Why did we win, Caleb?" Othniel repeats gently.

"Because the Lord God went before us into battle, and gave the Mesopotamians into our hands," he replies quietly. His young face is awed and reverent.

Othniel's face relaxes, and his smile is warm and approving. "Exactly, Caleb. And because He has done this for us, what do you think we should do?"

"Tear down every altar to Baal and Ashteroth in the land!" yells the soldier.

A loud roar of agreement erupts from every throat, and the group turns from the clearing to rush down the side of the hill. Othniel turns to Hannah, his expression kind.

"Come, Hannah," he says gently. "You have done good work this night—now let the young ones finish it. Let me take you to your home."

The two figures fade from sight in the leaping flames of the chariot of fire. As you take the reins thoughtfully in hand, you ask slowly, "Will the Israelites be oppressed anymore by the Mesopotamians?"

"No, little one," answers the musical voice. "They will have peace in the land for forty years, while Othniel is their judge. Now it is time for your next decision."

You listen carefully as the voice continues, "You may see Shamgar, another judge. Or you may see the Canaanites, another people who oppressed Israel."

Still wondering if the judges were legal experts, you think carefully and then pull the reins taut.

If you decide to see Shamgar, go to page 55.

If you decide to see the Canaanites, go to page 60.

(You Have Decided
to See the Moabites)

A fine mist clings to your hair and tunic as you gaze from a stone tower over fertile fields below. As far as you can see, neat squares of golden wheat fields gleam dully throught the mist, alternating with orchards bursting with fruit. You rest your forearms on the damp stone and watch sea gulls wheel overhead in the grey sky. You glance curiously behind you, and see that you are standing atop one of four round towers set in the corners of a small fortress. You climb slowly down narrow stone steps inside the dark tower, and cautiously edge out into the courtyard.

Soldiers hurry in every direction and donkeys jostle each other in the center of the courtyard. Burnished shields line the walls, and wicked-looking swords hang at each soldier's side.

"Here!" shouts a soldier, pointing to you. "Come with me!"

You fall into step obediently behind him, as he strides through the open gates of the fortress. A wide road, filled with ox-drawn carts, donkeys, and people passes in front of the fortress. The soldier surveys the crowd impatiently.

"Let me through!" he commands sharply, his hand on the sword at his side.

Wide-eyed, the people make a path for the soldier, who swaggers confidently through the throng. You hurry behind him and see that the broad roadway stretches straight through the tilled fields toward stone walls on the distant plain. The carts around you are filled with bulging sacks and baskets of grain.

"Is everyone taking their grain to the city to sell?" you ask the soldier.

"To sell!" he snorts. "Of course not! That is tribute they are bringing to King Eglon. The Israelites would not *dare* sell what they must bring to our king!" He glances down at you impatiently. "Anyway, that is no city ahead of us—that is the palace of the king of Moab. Have you never traveled on the king's highway before?" he asks suspiciously.

You shake your head nervously, hoping with all your heart that the soldier will not ask you where you are from. He says nothing, but quickens his pace until you must almost run to keep up with him. He brushes past a tall cloaked figure who leads a donkey loaded with sacks of grain. The soldier flicks a careless glance toward the man, then walks on, but for some reason your eyes are drawn to the man's face. You see wrath blaze in his eyes for an instant and then disappear. Something about this man is exciting!

You and the soldier cross the distance to the palace and pass through the open gates of the palace wall into a large courtyard. Palm trees cluster around a central fountain, their leaves shining dully in the mist.

"Help the Israelites carry their tribute to the king," the soldier commands you curtly. Wheeling around, he stares hard at the mysterious cloaked figure. "There is something about you that I don't like, you Hebrew dog!" the soldier sneers.

"Ehud!" a voice gasps. "The soldier is talking to you!"

The man steps forward confidently, his eyes meeting the soldier's suspicious stare. "I am Ehud, of the tribe of Benjamin," he says quietly.

You jump nervously as the soldier draws his sword, using the point to lift the folds of cloak away from Ehud's left side. "No sword on your hip, Benjamite! You may thank your gods I did not find one. I mistrust those fierce eyes of yours!"

A strange expression flickers in Ehud's eyes, then

dies quickly. Waves of relief wash over you as you hoist a heavy skin bag onto your shoulder and follow the crowd through the wooden doors of the palace. All struggle in with their tribute, laying it at the foot of the throne of the king of Moab. You heave your sack to the ground, darting a curious look at the king. You struggle to keep your face expressionless, for there on the throne is the most grotesquely fat man you have ever seen in your life! Huge rolls of fat cascade from chin down, and his eyes peer out of slits in his swollen face.

Heaving his enormous bulk up out of the throne, the king glances at Ehud.

"When you have finished bringing in the tribute," Ehud says quietly to his fellow Israelites, "you may leave this place." Ehud turns to the king, his level gaze unafraid. "I have a secret message for you, O king."

Interest sparkles in the king's beady eyes, and he moves ponderously toward stone steps leading upward. "You need not follow," says the king to his waiting soldiers. "I am in no danger from an Israelite!" he sneers.

The last Israelite hurries out of the audience hall, and Ehud calmly follows the Moabite king up the broad stone steps. You creep silently behind them, listening in horrified fascination as the king wheezes up the stairs. At last you reach the landing, and peer around the corner into a cool and shadowy porch. Ehud and the king are vanishing into a small room at one end, and you tiptoe forward to look inside.

The Moabite king has settled his tremendous

bulk on a stone bench in the shadows. Ehud leans forward, saying quietly, "I have a message from God for you."

You see the king's eyes widen and he starts to get to his feet, staring fixedly at Ehud. In one fluid motion, Ehud whips back the folds of his cloak with his right hand revealing a gleaming sword strapped to his right thigh. His left hand draws the sword, and he plunges it into the king. You press your hand against your mouth to keep from shrieking, for the king is so enormous that the eighteen-inch long sword has completely disappeared, handle and all, into the mountains of fat.

Ehud springs back, his eyes blazing. He backs swiftly out onto the porch, carefully drawing the doors shut behind him. Turning the key in the lock, his glance travels over you swiftly as he bounds across the small porch to the staircase. You stand uncertainly as Ehud disappears down the stairs. Should you remain here to see what happens next, or should you follow Ehud?

If you decide to stay with the king, go to page 42.

If you decide to follow Ehud, go to page 43.

(You Have Decided
to Stay With the King of Moab)

The sound of Ehud's footsteps dies away, and you discover that your knees are shaking. You had not expected Ehud to kill the king of Moab right before your eyes, and your senses reel crazily. You know that the Moabites oppressed Israel—but did the king of Moab deserve death at Ehud's hand? Suddenly you remember that the archive had something to say about the Moabites, and you draw it from your sash with trembling hands.

Unrolling the scroll carefully, you scan it until you find the part that says the Moabites were known as the people of Chemosh—a god who was worshiped by burning children! Overcome with revulsion, you realize that in every culture a king was expected to lead his people in worship—King Eglon would have committed terrible wickedness! You roll the scroll up hastily and tuck it back into your sash.

Suddenly the enormity of your situation dawns on you. You are standing here, alone—and on the other side of the door is the murdered king of Moab! What would you say if his servants discovered you here with his body? A pulse throbs in your temple, and you decide that you had better get out of here before you are accused of murder!

Go to page 43.

(You Have Decided to Follow Ehud)

Your heart hammering, you dash toward the stone stairs. Willing yourself to be calm, you deliberately slow your steps, reaching the throne room just as the cloaked figure of Ehud vanishes through the doorway. The sacks of grain are still stacked at the foot of the throne, and soldiers are everywhere.

A vise-like grip of a Moabite soldier fastens painfully on your shoulder, and you look cautiously into the man's hard grey eyes. "What is the king doing up there?" he growls. "The Benjamite did not spend much time with him!"

"The king is in his chamber," you reply—grateful that your voice does not reveal your terror. "The doors of his chamber are closed. How should I know what he is doing?" you shrug carelessly.

"Begone, you Israelite dog!" snarls the soldier. "I have seen enough of your kind for one day!"

Relief turns your legs to water, but you obey swiftly—you'd like nothing better than to get out of this place! You burst out of the room, searching anxiously for Ehud. At last you see him, and you elbow your way toward his retreating back. Once outside the palace walls, Ehud breaks into a trot toward low hills in the distance. You jog after him.

"Ehud! Wait!" you call, as he disappears in a grove of trees at the foot of the hill. You know that you will never find him in unfamiliar terrain—he could be lost from your sight in seconds.

Your eyes strain and your chest is heaving, but you run on, until your foot catches in a hole and you fall heavily to the ground at the edge of the trees. Almost sobbing in disappointment, you clamber to your feet—wincing in pain as you put weight on your twisted ankle.

"Here, my friend," a low voice issues from the grove beyond.

You limp toward the sound, pain shooting up your leg with every step. Ehud steps suddenly out from behind a tree, his face concerned. Supporting you in one strong arm, he leads you slowly toward a boulder. You collapse onto the flat boulder, while Ehud kneels on the ground. He takes your ankle gently in one hand, peering carefully at it.

"Nothing broken," he says cheerfully. "It will be sore without a doubt—but you may walk on it. You do not have the look of a Moabite, so you may come with me if you wish," he adds with a smile.

You nod gratefully, hoping that you will learn something that might help you on your quest. He helps you to your feet and together you walk slowly through the grove. After some time you break the companionable silence. "Did God appoint you to be a judge?" you ask curiously.

Ehud stares at you. "A judge?" he questions. "I don't know anything about that. I only know that God will deliver the Moabites into our hands!" His thick brows meet in a frown, and his eyes flash with anger. "The Lord God has warned us over and over in the past! When will the people learn?"

"Warned you about what?" you ask.

A snort of disgust bursts from the man. "You would think that Israel would not wish to worship useless gods, when the one true God led our people out of captivity in Egypt! How dare anyone so blessed worship idols made of stone who call for the bloody sacrifice of children? Israel has done evil in the sight of our God — and He has warned us that if we turn from Him, He will deliver us into the hands of our enemies!"

"But surely not *every* Israelite worshiped pagan gods?" you say slowly.

"Oh no! But many have taken Moabite wives, which we are forbidden to do," Ehud replies.

You puzzle over this, then ask, "But why does it matter who an Israelite marries, as long as he or she continues to worship God?"

Ehud stops, placing both arms on your shoulders and frowning soberly. "This is the reason, my friend — listen well. When a person marries, he or she wishes above all else to please his or her spouse. So it becomes easy to think, 'What does it matter if my mate wishes to offer just a little sacrifice to Chemosh? How can that hurt?'" He paces furiously and continues, "Soon there are children, and how can they know that there is only one God when they see their parents worshiping more? So they fall into the easiest path, and the ways of the idol worshipers give much pleasure. Who will want to follow the one true God when they can enjoy the wicked priestesses of Astarte, or take part in the bloody orgies of Baal?"

"I see!" you exclaim. "It wouldn't take very long before no one would even *know* about God anymore!"

"Exactly!" Ehud shouts triumphantly. "Israel would cease to exist. I'm afraid that it is only when my people are oppressed that they remember the

Lord, so He allows us to fall into the hands of our enemies. But when will we *learn*?" he groans.

Ehud turns to you. "The Lord has told me to gather the Israelites; He will give the Moabites into our hands. Do you wish to come with me, or do you wish to stay hidden here?"

Out of the corner of your eye you see the radiant flames of your chariot in the darkest corner of the thick grove of trees. "I think that I will stay here," you reply.

Ehud smiles kindly. "Then farewell, and may you remember the Lord our God all your days!" He strides swiftly away, disappearing almost immediately into the green shadows. You dart through the trees, scrambling into the waiting chariot.

"Here are your choices," chimes the voice. "I may take you almost eighty years into the future, where you may learn if Israel continued to be oppressed by the Moabites while Ehud was Israel's judge. Or I may take you a short distance into the future, to see the Moabites delivered into Israel's hands. What is your decision?"

Thinking carefully, you make your choice.

If you decide to go eighty years into the future, go to page 51.

If you decide to see Israel defeat the Moabites, go to page 47.

(You Have Decided to See Israel Defeat the Moabites)

A trumpet blast shudders in the early morning air and echoes from distant green hills. You are standing beneath a small tree that overhangs a river. The sound of rushing water is loud, and you notice with interest that a dead branch on the surface of the water speeds past you; the current must be treacherously swift here. You look west across a flat, sandy plain — palm trees rise skyward in the distance, and you *think* you can see city walls shimmering in the heat. Wiping the sweat from your forehead with the back of your hand, you wonder how it can be so hot so early in the morning!

A growing rumble rises in volume, and you scan both sides of the river quickly — seeing nothing. You step out from beneath the scrubby little tree and strike out into the flat desert just beyond. Your heart leaps into your throat, for now you see what has made the rumble: Hundreds of armed Israelites are marching toward you, swords in hand. The faces confronting you are grim, and you can see leather quivers full of arrows hanging over the men's shoulders.

You search anxiously for Ehud, and see him at last; he has withdrawn a short way from the ranks and is raising a polished ram's horn to his lips. The long, low blast that follows sends chills down your spine — for you know that Ehud must be giving the signal for war. You jog quickly toward his side, resolving to stay by him if you can.

The first ranks of soldiers have already waded into the rushing river. "Beware the current!" Ehud calls sharply. "Remember—no Moabite is to be allowed to ford the Jordan!"

Your heart begins to pound as the river grows nearer, and you press closer to Ehud's side. At last you are plunging into the racing water, feeling the raging current tugging hard at your legs. Suddenly, your foot slips on a rock and water rushes into your mouth as you slip beneath the surface. Tearing at you mercilessly, the current forces you downriver; your lungs feel as if they must burst. A hand fastens on your hair, pulling you up and out of the water—and you gulp deeply, filling your lungs with air. Coughing and sputtering, you look directly into the face of Ehud.

He smiles sympathetically. "I'm glad I was able to rescue you—again!" he whispers with a low chuckle as he releases your hair, and you find safe footing. "You will see us defeat the Moabites this day—for the Lord will give them into our hands!" His eyes flash as he looks at the opposite bank of the river.

You scramble gratefully onto dry land, stopping beneath a low tree to wring the water out of your tunic. Glancing up, you are startled to see hundreds of Moabite soldiers marching directly toward the Israelites.

"Remember the Lord our God!" roars Ehud. A deadly battle cry erupts from every throat and both armies head toward each other at a run. Metal-tipped arrows fly through the air, and you see Moabites fall heavily. A swift glance assures you

that so far, no Israelite has fallen! Ehud's men surge past you and you see the real battle begin at a point about two hundred yards from the east bank of the Jordan river.

Leaping flames surround you and you see the battle no more.

"Will Ehud's men really win?" you ask quietly.

"Yes, little one," answers the steed. "Ten thousand Moabites will be slain this day—and Moab will oppress Israel *no more* from this day forth.

"Now it is again time for you to make a decision. I am allowed to take you to learn more about the Canaanites, who oppressed Israel. Or you may choose to see Deborah, who judged Israel during the Canaanite oppression." The voice falls silent.

You remember that part of your quest is to find out *why* God appointed judges—and you still have no idea of the answer. Wondering which choice might help you more, you take the reins thoughtfully in hand and pull them taut.

**If you decide to see Deborah,
go to page 67.**

**If you decide to see the Canaanites,
go to page 59.**

(You Have Decided to Go
Eighty Years Into the Future)

A bird trills joyously in the branches above you, and you look up through rustling leaves at an intensely blue sky. Bees drone sleepily nearby, and you see grapevines heavy with near-bursting fruit growing riotously behind a whitewashed home. An old man, his wispy white hair a halo around his head, sits on a wooden bench in front of the house. You walk slowly toward him, thinking over what you might ask.

"Greetings, stranger!" the old man calls, his face crinkling into a smile of welcome. "What a day our God has given us! Come and sit beside me," he says, patting the bench invitingly.

You return his smile and sink down onto the bench, leaning back against the sun-warmed stone of the house. Peace washes over you and you close your eyes for a moment while you listen to the soothing symphony of birds and bees.

The old man sighs contentedly. "How Israel has prospered since Ehud rose up to be our judge. Youngsters of your age have no idea of the terror of Moabite oppression! And I thank our God that you don't!" he adds with gusto.

"Doesn't Israel have to pay tribute to Moab anymore?" you question eagerly.

A rich laugh rumbles deep in the man's chest. "Oh no, youngster—we have not paid tribute since Ehud and his men defeated the Moabites at the fords of the Jordan, almost eighty years ago. Ten thousand Moabites fell at the hands of Israelites on that day!"

"*Ten thousand*!" you exclaim in surprise.

He nods vigorously. "I remember it well—even though I was but a lad. The Moabites outnumbered our forces and their weapons were vastly superior—but the Lord God went before us, and we won! Ehud made certain that every Israelite knew *why* we had been victorious—and Israel turned from wickedness to worship the God of our fathers once more! Ah!" he sighs happily. "The worship of God is as refreshing as cool water on a hot day. Perhaps I should not tell you this," he says as his voice sinks to a conspiratorial whisper, "but my favorite festival begins at sunset tonight!"

You cannot help smiling as you look at his weathered old face, wreathed in smiles. The old man chuckles happily.

"Booths! I love this time!" he murmurs. "Moses set the festival, that all generations may remember that God made the children of Israel live in booths when He brought them out of Egypt. Will you stay?" he asks, suddenly twisting around on the bench to grasp your arm urgently. "I would love to welcome you to our family's celebration!"

You hesitate, wondering if you will be allowed to stay; you would hate to hurt this gentle old man's feelings.

He rushes into speech once more. "We shall sleep out-of-doors in our booth, under the stars. We shall feast, and sing, and have a wonderful time as we remember what the Lord our God has done for Israel!" The old man's eyes flash with anticipation, then suddenly swim with tears. "But fewer and fewer celebrate each year! I pray that my people are not beginning to fall into evil ways once again." He subsides into silence, his once-happy expression dimmed with worry. Somehow the bright golden day seems clouded by the invisible presence of evil—and you shiver suddenly in spite of the sunshine.

The radiant flames of the chariot of fire glow all around you, and the old man's face disappears.

"Is he right?" you ask breathlessly. "Is Israel falling into wickedness again?"

A short pause seems like an eternity until the voice answers sadly, "Yes, little one. For eighty years Israel was undisturbed—but then they once again began to worship idols."

Your heart is wrenched at the thought of the old man's delight in worship turning to agony. "Will he see the evil return?" you ask softly.

"No, my friend—the Lord will gather him to his fathers to spare him that sorrow. He has delighted in the Lord, and he will go home soon. Now I will take you to see the Canaanites—a people who oppressed Israel. Mark well what you learn there."

Here goes! you think in excitement as you pick up the reins and wait.

Go to page 59.

(You Have Decided to See Shamgar)

A wildly-barking dog faces you, his attitude fierce. You back away slightly, intending to show him that you mean no harm. His barks subside, and as you extend your hand toward him, palm up, the scruffy little animal wags his tail uncertainly. You find you are standing in front of a small stone house, its irregular stones apparently set into mud and then whitewashed. A little boy in front of the house stares wide-eyed at you—his gaze fearful and anxious. The door of the house bursts open, and a woman darts out, scooping the little boy into her arms.

"What do you want, young stranger?" she asks, her voice shaking slightly. "Please do not take our last goat," she continues. "The Philistines have left us only one—will you take even that?"

"No, no!" you answer hurriedly, your heart wrung by her desperation. "I would never do such a thing! Why would anyone want to steal your goats?"

The woman pushes a stray lock of hair away from her eyes with the back of a work-worn hand. She sets the little boy back down on the ground with a weary sigh. "The Philistines steal our goats to sacrifice to their god, Dagon." She shudders, her tired face twisting in horror. "One of their strongest cities is not far from here, and it is easy for them to take what they want from any Israelite! My husband says that the Israelites are oppressed by the Philistines because as a people we have forgotten God... and I think he is right!" she adds, her jaw set

in brave determination. "But, I forget my manners," the woman says with a smile. "Please come into our home — we do not have much, but you are welcome to what we have."

The little boy tugs your tunic urgently, his trusting brown eyes sparkling up at you. You cannot help smiling as he pulls you into the house. Once inside, you look around at a small courtyard; a fire glows cheerfully in the stone oven in the center. Tall clay jars line one side of the courtyard, and four arched doorways are set in the walls.

The little boy toddles over to the oven and plops himself onto the ground. You sit beside him, and the woman pours you both a frothy cup of milk from a nearby jug.

"My husband would want you to share our meal," says the woman, a crease of worry appearing between her brows. "I am hoping that he will be home soon."

"My father has gone to slay some Philistines!" crows the little boy with pride. "Already he has slain more than five hundred with his ox goad!"

You glance swiftly at the woman, seeing a look of fear mingled with pride flit across her face. "Yes, Shamgar is a brave man," she says in answer to your inquiring gaze. "Each day, after his work is finished, he goes to help other Israelites who have suffered at the hands of the Philistines. I do not know what I would do without him, but I know that he does what must be done to save Israel!" Tears tremble on the woman's dark lashes, but her face is full of love.

The sound of men's voices penetrates the quiet

courtyard, and the woman's face drains of color. Before you can even scramble to your feet, the wooden door bursts open—and a throng of exuberant men surge into the room.

"Shamgar! You are safe!" the woman sobs, rushing across the courtyard to fling her arms around the neck of a ruddy-faced Israelite.

Each man's face is wreathed in smiles. "Your husband has saved Israel!" shouts a young man triumphantly. "Six hundred Philistines have fallen at Shamgar's hands! We may live in peace for a long time, I think—even the Philistines of Gath will pause before they bother us again!"

The little boy claps his hands in excitement. "Ooooh! The men of Gath are giants—huge, tall men!"

"Yes, little fellow!" laughs Shamgar, affectionately scooping up his little son to hold him high in the air. "That is no tale—the men grow tall as trees in Gath!"

Men surge around Shamgar, and you notice one holding a staff about eight feet long which ends in a sharp metal tip. The man holding it nods proudly as he sees you eyeing it. "Yes indeed! This very goad is what Shamgar used to rid us of the Philistine curse!"

Shamgar puts his son gently down and raises his hand to call for attention. The excited buzz of voices dies and the men look at him expectantly.

"Listen, Israel!" says Shamgar soberly. "The Lord has delivered us from the Philistines. We must never forget God, who delivered our grandfathers from bondage in Egypt, and who brought us to this bountiful land. We are the children of Abraham, Isaac, and Jacob—we are His people!"

The men's faces are serious as they listen intently.

"Hear, 0 Israel: The Lord our God is one Lord!" thunders Shamgar. "Moses told our grandfathers to love the Lord God with all their heart and soul and might. We are to teach our children about God, to talk of Him when we sit in our house, and when we walk, and when we lie down, and when we arise."

The men's voices rise together in a swelling chorus, "Hear, O Israel: The Lord our God is one Lord!"

The ancient words of praise seem to echo from the walls, and you feel both awed and humble as the leaping flames of the chariot surround you.

"Here is your choice," chimes the musical voice. "I may take you to see the Moabites, a people who also oppressed Israel. Or I may take you to a temple in Haran—a city in Mesopotamia. Which will you choose?"

Uncertainly, you pick up the smooth leather reins. Wondering which destination might help you more, you make your decision quickly.

If you decide to see the Moabites, go to page 36.

If you decide to see a temple in Haran, go to page 27.

(You Have Decided to
See the Canaanites)

Oil lamps glow softly against the pale-yellow stone walls of a large room. Shadows flicker on the floor, which is a vibrant mosaic of colored seashells. A man and a woman sit facing each other across a table, their excited conversation rising and falling in contrast to the soft harp melody that floats in the air. A servant approaches their table and bows before placing a large, decorated jar between them. Two long reeds extend from the jar and the woman delicately lifts one of them into her mouth and uses it to sip some of the beverage.

Well, how about that! you think. *Who'd have guessed that people used drinking straws over three thousand years ago!* You wonder if this couple is wealthy, for their clothing is richly embroidered, and bracelets and earrings of gold flash from the woman's arms and ears.

"I am concerned about my ship that sets sail tomorrow," says the man with a heavy frown. "It carries a valuable load—one which will make us rich beyond our dreams!"

The woman pushes her glossy black hair impatiently back from her face. "I am also concerned, husband," she snaps. "We have discussed this

before. This venture is much too important to leave to chance; we *must* offer sacrifice to the great god Baal. Only he can assure safe passage of this cargo!"

Holding his hand up wearily, the man shakes his head slowly. "I know, I know. But our first-born child? Surely another sacrifice would do just as well!"

"You would withhold this sacrifice to the great Baal, when our whole future depends upon it?" the woman questions, her voice rising shrilly.

Chills wash over you as you listen—surely you have misunderstood! *They cannot be talking about sacrificing a child to Baal!*

Gusty wails suddenly echo from a distant hallway, coming closer every second. As you watch in growing horror, a servant enters the room carrying a tiny baby who is squalling at the top of his lungs.

"Here is the child, my lady," says the servant woodenly, holding the child out to her.

The woman's eyes flick carelessly over the baby, then fix intently on her husband's face. "Well, husband? Make your decision!"

The man turns away from the child, his mouth twisted. "Very well," he replies. "Have the child taken to the temple."

The servant hurries away from the table, spotting you suddenly in the shadows. He thrusts the baby into your arms. "Here!" he barks. "The child is to be taken to the temple of Baal—see that you do not delay! And remember," he hisses. "Tell the priest your master's name, and the purpose of the sacrifice."

You stumble blindly from the room, clutching the wailing child to your chest. You find yourself out on the street, not knowing how you got there or what to do next. Your heart is hammering and your stomach churning. You lift a corner of the soft blanket and confront the wide stare of a very young baby. He stops crying and regards you with a startled look, lifting a tentative little arm toward your nose.

Your brain reels, for you remember very clearly that the rules of travel tell you that you cannot change history in any way; but how can you have any part in taking this little one to his death? The streets are teeming with people and you huddle against the stone wall of the house, wondering how you are going to be able to save this baby's life. You must find a safe home for him—but how?

A glance down the street shows you the city walls in the distance, and you remember that Israelites lived in Canaan. If you could find them, somehow—surely one of them would take this little one into their family. Shifting the baby more comfortably in your arms, you start down the dusty street at a fast trot. You've got to get out of this horrible city before anyone can stop you!

At last you burst through the city gates, spotting a grove of trees off the road in the distance. Running for all you're worth, you head for the grove—and notice in the back of your mind that the footsteps that were behind you in the city are still following; whoever it is is now running as fast as you are. Sparing no look over your shoulder, you reach the grove of trees. Gasping for breath, you resolve that you will defend this baby with your own life if you must—and you search the ground wildly for some kind of weapon. Seeing a large jagged rock, you bend swiftly to seize it and whirl around, clutching the baby in one arm. Wielding the sharp stone in the other hand, you raise your arm to strike your pursuer.

A young man stares fiercely at you as you shout between gasps, "Stop right there! You cannot take this baby for Baal unless you kill me first!"

His eyes widen and you tense to spring. The young man steps back from you, an odd smile flickering on his lips. "I do not want to take the baby to the temple of Baal," he replies. "I was planning to rescue him—but you beat me to it!"

"What?" you ask warily, tightening your hold on the baby and your weapon.

A warm smile lights his face. "I am an Israelite,

captured by the Canaanites several years ago. I have been a slave in the house where you were since I was a boy. All that time, I have been faithful to God. The master of the house trusts me, and I could have escaped before this, but something told me to wait."

You relax a little, leaning against the rough bark of a tree at your back. The baby squirms in your tight grip, and you loosen your hold. "Go on," you urge.

"My master was proud of his firstborn child and he loved him. But many wealthy merchants and noblemen have sacrificed their firstborn to Baal—and my lady was certain that the sacrifice would insure their continued wealth!" The young man's voice is bitter, and his eyes glitter with disgust. "As soon as I heard the rumors, I made my plans. For the last two weeks, I have been saving bits and scraps of food, to last on the journey. I had planned to take the baby tonight, and escape to my people. I have hidden my satchel in this very grove of trees—all was ready."

"And then?" you breathe.

He grins. "And then—you! I crept into the baby's room just in time to see the servant take him to the dining hall. I'll say this for you—you're a swift runner!" he laughs ruefully.

With a sigh of relief, you look once more at the baby in your arms. "Will you be able to find a family to take care of him?" you ask carefully — you feel responsible for this little fellow, and need to be certain he'll be safe.

The young man smiles. "My mother will love him, even if he is a Canaanite baby! And I will teach him myself about the Lord God who remembers His servants. Don't worry my friend — this baby will be loved and cared for!" He reaches for the baby, and tucks him expertly in the crook of his arm. "I must hurry now — I wish to put a lot of distance between us and the city before the sun sets. May the Lord God bless you!" he says softly as he hoists a satchel over his shoulder.

As he turns away, the flames of the chariot dance all around you. Relieved at the outcome of this particular adventure, you listen in growing excitement for the voice of the magnificent steed.

"Do you understand now why the Lord God told the Israelites to drive the Canaanites out of the land?" asks the voice softly.

You shudder, and nod vigorously.

"Then I am allowed to take you now to see Deborah, who judged Israel during the Canaanite oppression," says the steed.

A woman judge? you wonder in surprise. Eagerly you take the reins in your hands and wait.

Go to page 67.

(You Have Come to See Deborah)

Angry voices hurl accusations, shattering the peace of the beautiful morning. You find yourself standing in a grove of palm trees, dates ripe to bursting beneath their branches. Low green hills stretch as far as you can see, and sheep dot the landscape. Beneath a palm tree several feet away sits a woman, her head slightly bent to one side as she listens intently to two men arguing violently. You walk slowly toward the trio and suddenly, the woman stands. She raises one small hand to stem the furious stream of accusations—and to your amazement, both men are silenced.

"Enough arguing!" Deborah's soft voice is soothing, yet commanding. "Do you think that the Lord God would wish His people to be quarreling among themselves?"

Both men hang their heads in shame, and surprise washes over you—for Deborah is a tiny woman, yet her gentle voice is compelling all the same. You can't picture any two men from your own time being silenced by such a small, softvoiced woman! You walk around the group to catch a glimpse of Deborah's face.

"I have heard your quarrel," she says slowly. "Here is my judgement. You dispute over ownership of land—yet neither of you can prove the land is his."

One of the men opens his mouth to argue, but stops as Deborah motions him to be still. You look at her in fascination—and understand instantly why these men obey Deborah. Her face is lit by an inner glow both loving and stern; she has a special quality of holiness which strikes you so forcibly that you are almost breathless in the face of it.

At last! you reflect, *here is a judge actually giving a verdict!*

"God is not honored by your strife," she says severely. "From this day forward, you will remember to honor the Lord your God as you *share* the land in peace. Do not forget that all things in the heavens and the earth come from Him. Both of you must dedicate to Him the best of His gifts from the land that He has given to you."

The men turn to each other sheepishly. "I guess we could share the land with no trouble," mumbles one.

A wail startles all of you, and you watch as a sturdy little boy hurtles up the gentle slope. Tears have traced paths through the dirt on his face, and his lower lip is swollen and bleeding. His chubby legs labor up the slope, which is steep for the toddler. The men smile affectionately as the little boy flings himself against Deborah.

Deborah bends tenderly over him, her hand resting comfortingly on his tousled curls. "What is it, little son?"

The little boy backs away, his face mutinous. He scowls ferociously, struggling not to cry. "They laughed at me!" he roars, his face red with rage at the memory. "I told them you had sent me to fetch Barak—and they said I wouldn't even know where to find him! But I *did!*" he finishes, his plump jaw jutting in determination.

Deborah places her hands on the shoulders of the

child, and shakes him gently. "Of course you did! I knew you would be able to do what I asked. You did very well, my son—for here is Barak now!"

A burly man toils up the slopes, his weathered face crinkling into a smile as he looks up to see Deborah. "Your little lad found me on the road," he says as he glances at the child with a twinkle. "He directed me how to find you very well—although I'm afraid he ran into a little battle of his own first!" Barak's face grows serious as he looks at Deborah. "You summoned me?" he asks soberly.

Deborah looks at Barak calmly. "The Lord God has commanded, 'Go and march to Mount Tabor, and take with you ten thousand men from the sons of Naphtali and from the sons of Zebulun.'"

Barak stares incredulously as Deborah's soft voice continues, "And the Lord will draw out to you Sisera, the commander of Jabin's army, with his chariots and his many troops, to the river Kishon; and the Lord will give him into your hand."

A low whistle of surprise erupts from one of the men whom Deborah has judged. "Deborah is sending Barak out to do battle with the Canaanites!" he whispers.

"If you will go with me, then I will go; but if you will not go with me, I will not go," says Barak simply.

Deborah looks at him for a moment, then says gently, "I will surely go with you. But the honor will not be yours on the journey that you are about to take, for the Lord will sell Sisera into the hands of a woman."

The little boy's hand steals into the large hand of

Barak. The burly warrior smiles absently at the child, and the three begin to walk slowly down the hill. You edge closer to the two men who have stayed, and who are obviously bursting with excitement.

"This means our long oppression by the evil Canaanites is finished!" exults one. "The Lord God is going to deliver us!"

His companion nods. "Twenty years we have suffered at their hands! Praise be to the Lord God for His deliverance!"

They hurry off together, disappearing from sight as the flames of the chariot engulf you. You reflect carefully on what you have just seen: even though Deborah gave a verdict in a quarrel, like twentieth-century judges, you are really beginning to think that a judge over Israel involved a whole lot more than that!

"Here is your choice," the voice of the magnificent steed breaks gently into your thoughts. "You may see Barak's victory over the Canaanites at Megiddo, or you may see what happens to Sisera, the Canaanite general."

Your thoughts whirling, you make your decision swiftly.

If you decide to see Barak's victory, go to page 72.

If you decide to see what happens to Sisera, go to page 78.

(You Have Decided
to See Barak's Victory)

Gusts of wind tear at your tunic, whipping it tightly around you. You inhale deeply, smelling the sharp scent of pine trees. A bolt of lightning splits the sky and the air shudders at the rumbles of thunder that follow. Banks of slate-grey clouds tumble over each other as they scud across the sky. From your vantage point high above the plain, the fields below look like a giant's checker-board in green and gold. The river winding its way between the fields reflects the sky's grey.

"Look down there!" a quiet voice speaks in your ear. You turn to see Deborah, her face alive with triumph. Looking in the direction of her pointing finger, you search the valley below.

Hundreds of chariots and thousands of men spill through a narrow gap in the low mountain range in the distance, following the river. You shiver in the cooling air, watching the advance of the Canaanite army. "How will you defeat them?" you whisper in awe. "They have *chariots* —how can the Israelite foot soldiers fight them?"

Deborah throws back her head in a delighted laugh. "The Lord God will deliver them into our hands—you will see!" She whirls around, and cups her hands around her mouth. "Barak—

arise!" she calls, her voice throbbing against the wind.

The ground beneath your feet trembles as a deafening crack of lightning rends the darkening sky. Drops of rain fall, first a few—and then sheets of water suddenly pour from the sky toward the plain.

"This is the day in which the Lord has given Sisera into your hands: behold, the Lord has gone out before you!" cries Deborah.

Barak strides into view, his face grim with determination. Falling into place behind him, their swords unsheathed, are young men and old—all with the light of battle in their eyes. As you watch, still more men stream through the trees. Not all have swords, and many carry only their leather slings with a pouch over their shoulders to hold the stones. Torrents of rain drive Barak's men down the steep mountain slope, straight toward the Canaanite troops.

You scramble down the incline, catching hold of a young pine tree as your feet slip on the slippery rocks. Glancing back over your shoulder, you see men still pouring over the crest of the hill. The wind and rain propel you mercilessly down until at last—panting and exhausted—you stand on the flat plain. Squinting into the deluge of wind-whipped rain, you see Barak's men have descended the mountain at an angle, reaching the

plain much farther toward the chariots than where you are standing. Shouts of alarm are snatched by the wind and thrown from mountain to mountain, echoing strangely in the storm's din.

Your pulse racing with excitement, you begin to run toward the battle. The river foams and churns, its grey waters swirling around boulders and uprooting small trees in its path as it rages over its banks. Mud begins to tug at your feet, slowing your progress. Your lungs feel as though they must burst from effort, and your steps slow.

Now you see that the Canaanite horses are rearing in front of their chariots, which are hopelessly stuck in the mire of mud. All is a confusion of shouts and flailing hooves, as frenzied charioteers crack their whips desperately across their horses' backs in an effort to free their vehicles from the mud. Barak's men are approaching the panicked Canaanites now, and with the clash of swords, the armies meet.

Flames and the silvery silence of the chariot engulf you, but your ears are still ringing with the sounds of battle. *How easily the Lord God destroyed the Canaanites' advantage over the Israelites!* you think. Somehow you know that Barak and his men will win this battle!

"Are you ready for your next choice?" asks the voice quietly. You nod eagerly, and the steed continues, "Then here it is; you may see the Philistines, who oppressed Israel for forty long years, or you may see the Midianites, who oppressed her for seven."

You suddenly remember that it was Samson who delivered Israel from the Philistines—how exciting it would be to actually see Samson! On the other hand, you are pretty certain that there was something equally exciting about the Midianites. Uncertain which choice would help you more, you hold the reins loosely until you make up your mind.

If you decide to see the Philistines, go to page 118.

If you decide to see the Midianites, go to page 82.

(You Have Decided to See
What Happens to Sisera)

A woman stands silhouetted against the twilight sky, her hands on her hips. A faint breeze stirs the hem of her tunic as she gazes into the distance. A huge tent squats at the foot of a rise, its dark shape almost blending in with the shadowed hill. One solitary star twinkles into life overhead, and an owl calls from far away.

"Have you seen Barak?" she questions sharply as she turns toward you.

"No, I haven't," you respond, a little startled by the woman's abrupt question.

She frowns, and you notice that her tunic is stained dark reddish brown. "I am certain that Barak would have pursued Sisera," she murmurs, more to herself than to you. "Surely he will be along soon!" She begins to pace impatiently. "I have never seen you before," the woman says suspiciously, "but you do not have the look of a Canaanite. I am Jael, wife of Heber the Kenite. And I am most blessed of women in the tent!" she exclaims, suppressed excitement throbbing in her voice.

Since you have no idea how to answer her, you struggle to look politely interested—not really very curious about why she is most blessed!

Jael grips your arm urgently, lowering her voice to a conspiratorial whisper. "I—a woman—have destroyed the general of the Canaanite army! How surprised Barak will be when he learns that Sisera is dead!"

Barely repressing a shudder, you agonize over what to say to this strange woman with her exultant smile. She seems to accept your silence as admiration, and rushes into speech again.

"The general never suspected me!" she whispers. "He was running away after his whole army was destroyed—and he thought he would find safety in my tent. Ha!" Jael laughs scornfully. "I lifted the tent peg while he slept, like so—" she raises her arm high above her head in a swift motion, her eyes glittering, "and drove it through his head with a hammer!"

Nauseated at the picture, you try not to let your horror show in your face—but Jael is not looking at you. She peers into the gathering gloom, then springs away from your side. Barak plods slowly toward her, and even in the dusk you can see utter weariness in his every movement.

The scene disappears as you find yourself back in the chariot of fire. Shuddering, you sink gratefully against the warm side.

"Something disturbs you, little one?" inquires the steed gently.

Mounting disgust makes you burst out, "*That was horrible*! Jael tricked him, and then murdered him! And she was *proud* of it!"

Miserably, you wait in the silence that follows. At last the gentle voice speaks once more.

"Would you rather have had the Canaanites destroy Israel? Would you have preferred that all knowledge of the Lord God be wiped out?"

"No, no!" you protest. "But murder is the worst of all sins, isn't it?"

"Where in the Word of God do you find sins ranked by degree, little one?" answers the steed. "Jael was an instrument in the hand of the Lord. The Canaanites' religion was totally wicked, and if they had continued to rule over Israel, eventually there would have been *no more Israel*. Jael was blessed because she was chosen by God to destroy

the Canaanite general.

"Now you will be allowed to see Barak's victory over the Canaanites," continues the voice.

You take the smooth leather reins in hand and wait.

Go to page 72.

(You Have Decided
to See the Midianites)

Wild whoops send chills racing down your spine and you whirl around to see where the dreadful sounds are coming from. You are standing in the midst of a field of golden-ripe grain at the foot of low, rocky hills. The thunder of approaching hoof-beats is growing closer, and you see a turbaned Midianite on the back of a camel galloping toward you . You search wildly for some place to hide, for the Midianite holds aloft a burning torch, its flames mirrored in his wicked eyes.

"Here—hurry!" whispers a voice. "Follow me!" You look down as you feel an urgent tug on the hem of your tunic and see a young man bent double—almost totally hidden amidst the shoulder-high grain. You drop swiftly into a crouch and follow him through the wheat field at the fastest pace you can manage. He zig-zags one way and then the other, heading generally toward the low hills. The whoops grow louder and fiercer, and the acrid smell of smoke assails your nostrils. You risk one glance over your shoulder to see more than twenty Midianites circling the field at a gallop on camel back, setting the field on fire. Panic seizes you by the throat as you realize that you no longer see the young man; you stumble blindly up the nearest hill.

You fall heavily as your feet slip on loose pebbles. Great plumes of smoke rise from the golden field while flames lick rapidly across the wheat. A cave entrance yawns in the shadow of the hill and the young man crouches at the entrance.

"Hurry!" he calls urgently as he pulls you inside. The moment you are inside the cave he pulls a scrubby bush in front of the entrance. With a sigh, he leans back against the wall of the cave. "What were you doing out there?" he scolds mildly. "Didn't you hear them coming?"

You shake your head, grateful to be out of the way of the Midianites at last. Your companion motions for you to follow and heads toward the back of the shallow cave. You follow curiously, just in time to see his feet disappear above! In the shadows at the back of the cave, a vertical shaft leads upward. The young man's face peers down at you from an opening above your head. Setting your feet carefully into notches in the stone, you climb up the shaft.

You step up into a larger cave, roughly twelve feet by twelve. The young man smiles proudly as he watches your eyes search the cave. "I am fortunate!" he says cheerfully. "The Lord God has blessed me with a fine home!"

Home! you reflect, with a sinking feeling. Several niches have been cut in the cave walls and covered clay pots are stored there. A worn woolen blanket is folded neatly in the corner atop a pile of rushes. In the center of the cave, a rock-ringed hole apparently serves as a well. The young man still regards you expectantly.

"Yes, you are fortunate," you reply with as convincing a smile as you can muster. "How long have you lived here?"

The young man gestures you grandly to have a

seat on the floor as he hustles over to a clay pot set in the wall. "Well," he begins as he rummages in the pot, "the Midianites drove our family out of our home about five years ago." Triumphantly he displays two small cakes he has found in the pot, then places them in a bowl and comes to squat beside you. Inviting you to serve yourself, he continues. "My family's cave is right beside mine—but I am going to take a wife soon, so I need a place of my own."

"Do all Israelites live in caves?" you ask carefully.

His eyes widen. "Not all, but *we* must," he replies. "You saw the Midianites today. We are never safe from them! They kill our oxen, steal our donkeys and sheep, and burn our fields. But at least while we live in dens, our lives are safe."

You frown over this for a moment. "How long have they been oppressing Israel?"

"Just about seven years," he murmurs. "But one of these days the Lord God will send someone to deliver us from the Midianites!" His eyes sparkle. "And if our deliverer has need of a warrior—here I am!"

You finish the cakes in companionable silence and take a long and refreshing drink of cool water which the young man has drawn from the well.

"Elihu!" calls a young voice from below.

The young man springs to his feet and disappears down the shaft. The cave is suddenly flooded with the shimmering flames of the chariot of fire, and you climb in behind the steed.

"Elihu is right," says the voice of the beautiful beast. "The Lord God will send the judge Gideon to deliver Israel from the Midianites. Here is your choice; you may see Gideon meet the angel of the Lord—or you may see what Gideon does after the angel leaves."

The music of the voice dies away, and you think carefully. *The angel of the Lord! Do I dare to make that choice?* On the other hand, you might have the chance to actually talk with Gideon if you choose the second course. At last you pick up the reins and make your decision.

If you decide to see the angel
of the Lord and Gideon, go to page 87.

If you decide to see what Gideon does
after the angel leaves, go to page 93.

(You Have Decided to See the Angel and Gideon)

You look downhill to see a fertile valley below; a silvery river winds its way through the valley toward the sea. Terraces of grain alternate with thick clusters of olive trees from the top of the hill almost to the river's edge. Several feet away from you, one solitary oak tree spreads luxuriant branches. You head toward it until you notice a figure sitting on a rock beneath it. Currents of excitement race through your veins making you tingle—the man looks perfectly ordinary, and yet . . . .

You find that you are slightly breathless, and with relief you hear an ordinary grunt. Turning in the direction of the sound, you see a man standing in a broad stone structure—something like a wide well. He is beating the ground fiercely, sweat streaming down his face. You walk closer, listening to the man mumble in irritation.

Rhythmically he beats the ground with a wooden shovel, and between each whack he complains. Whack! "What a fine situation for a man!" Whack! "Huddling in a winepress to beat the grain!" Whack! "I'll never be able to straighten my back again!" Whack! "Cursed Midianites!"

You eye him curiously, wondering why he is so cross. "What's wrong with beating grain in a winepress?" you ask.

Gideon drops his shovel. His eyes widen, then he stares at you reproachfully. "What's wrong with it? I'll tell you what's wrong. It's ridiculous!"

"Why?" you question.

Gideon picks up the shovel, leaning it carefully against the stone side of the winepress. He mops his streaming brow with a forearm and sighs. "A farmer would normally beat his wheat in a high, windy place—where the wind could carry away the chaff. But because of the Midianite threat, I have to crouch here like an animal—where the work of threshing is ten times harder with no wind to help me. I must save this wheat from the Midianites!" He spits the last words out angrily.

A powerful voice speaks suddenly, and you experience the same thrill of excitement you felt before. "The Lord is with you, O valiant warrior."

The figure that was beneath the tree is now standing just outside the winepress. Gideon stares at him in suspicion. "My lord, if the Lord is with us, why then has all this happened to us?" He climbs easily over the wall and faces the stranger. "And where are all His miracles which our fathers told us about, saying, 'Did not the Lord bring us up from Egypt?' But now the Lord has abandoned us and given us into the hand of Midian." Resentment grows in Gideon's voice as he sees that his words are having absolutely no effect upon the stranger.

"Go in this your strength and deliver Israel from the hand of Midian," says the man. More softly he adds, "Have I not sent you?" Infinite tenderness and love are in the low voice, and you feel awed and humbled.

Gideon's jaw juts stubbornly. "Lord, how shall I deliver Israel?" He lowers his eyes to the ground, murmuring miserably, "My family is the least in

Manasseh, and I am the least in my father's house."

"Surely I will be with you, and you shall defeat Midian as one man," says the voice.

After a long silence, Gideon raises his head. In his eyes, you see hope and fear struggling. He is pale, and he takes a deep breath before he speaks. "If now I have found favor in Thy sight, then show me a sign that it is Thou who speaks with me." His face terrified, Gideon's words tumble out. "Please do not depart from here until I come back to Thee, and bring out my offering and lay it before Thee."

The hair on the back of your neck rises. *Gideon is asking the angel of the Lord to wait right there?!*

The angel of the Lord speaks again, the patience of eternity in his strong voice. "I will remain until you return."

The flames engulf you in their dancing light and you find that you are shaking. The soft voice of the steed chimes musically. "I am allowed to give you two choices. You may wait at the winepress with the angel of the Lord, or you may go forward a few hours to see what Gideon does after the angel departs. Which will you choose?"

Taking the reins in your still-trembling hands, you make your decision.

If you decide to wait at the winepress, go to page 92.

If you decide to see what Gideon does, go to page 93.

(You Have Decided to Wait at the Winepress)

A cool evening breeze fans your cheeks as one lone star twinkles into life in the darkening sky. The oak tree is a black silhouette against the shadowy hillside and you see the angel of the Lord patiently waiting beneath the oak. In the gathering darkness, you see Gideon hurrying toward the tree, his hands full. Slowly you walk toward the two figures.

With a bow, Gideon offers the angel what he has brought—some meat in a basket, a pot of liquid of some kind, and flattened loaves of bread wrapped in rough cloth.

"Take the meat and the unleavened bread and lay them on this rock," says the angel of the Lord. "And pour out the broth."

Gideon hastily removes the meat from the basket, laying it carefully on the flat rock beneath the tree. Steam rises from the bread as Gideon unfolds the cloth and places the loaves beside the meat. After he has poured out the broth, he stands uncertainly—for there is an intense quiet—even the breeze seems to hold its breath.

The angel of the Lord stretches out his wooden staff, lightly touching the meat and bread. With a crackle, great curling tongues of fire leap up from the rock—Gideon's face is a white, terrified circle in the sudden glow of light. Leaping heavenward, the fire consumes the meal in a flash—and the angel of the Lord has vanished.

Go to page 93.

(You Have Come to See What Gideon Does After the Angel Departs)

Pale white clouds scud across a velvet night sky, and the moon bathes the hill in silvery radiance. Beneath a solitary oak tree, a man works feverishly piling stones on top of one another. You approach, watching Gideon's lips move silently as he works. He casts you a glance over his shoulder and gives you a gentle, welcoming smile.

Gideon's eyes are still wide with awe. "The name of this altar shall be Yahweh-Shalom—the Lord is Peace," he breathes. "I have seen the angel of the Lord in this very place, and yet I live!"

"Is this the only altar to the Lord in all the land of Israel?" you ask softly.

"Oh, no!" Gideon replies in horror, halting his work to gaze at you. "The main altar is, of course, at Shiloh—in the court of the tabernacle."

"The tabernacle!" you exclaim in surprise. "Do you mean that all these years after Moses, Israel still has the tabernacle? Is the ark of the covenant still inside?"

Gideon's brow wrinkles. "Well of course! Where else should it be?" He turns back to the altar, hands on hips as he regards it critically. "There," he murmurs in satisfaction.

Suddenly you are bathed in light as the flames of the chariot surround you. "Here is your choice," says the voice of the magnificent steed. "Gideon has yet another task to accomplish this night: He will tear down an altar to Baal. You may see Gideon tear down the altar, or you may see him seek a sign from the Lord that he is truly the Lord's choice to deliver Israel. Which will you choose?"

Pondering carefully, you pick up the reins and make your decision.

If you decide to see Gideon tear down Baal's altar, go to page 95.

If you decide to see Gideon seek a sign, go to page 99.

(You Have Decided to See Gideon Tear Down Baal's Altar)

A deafening crack splinters the chilly pre-dawn air, and you peer through the grey shadows to see a tall wooden pole crash to the ground. Triumphant shouts echo from several men, and you recognize Gideon staring down at the pole with a satisfied grin. You start forward, wincing in pain as you stumble on a large rock in your path. As your eyes grow accustomed to the colorless world just before dawn, you see that the flat hilltop is littered with crumbling rocks.

Gideon beckons you. "Look!" he shouts. "The altar of Baal is no more!"

You survey the rubble in astonishment. *This must have been quite a sizeable altar from the look of all the debris*! Picking your way through the rocks and crumbling mortar, you reach Gideon's side and ask curiously, "What is that pole?"

A grimace of disgust twists his features. "That *was* an Asherah pole—a tribute to Baal's lover. We shall use it for firewood in the altar we are building to the Lord God!"

You glance at the lewd scenes carved on the felled pole and feel disgust wash over you. Axes crash into the vile Asherah pole, and splinters fly. Time seems to stand still as Gideon and ten other men carefully build an altar, then place the firewood on top. Gideon gently places his hands on an ox tethered to a small tree nearby and then pulls a knife and ends its life with one swift, certain stroke.

Carefully he prepares the animal for sacrifice, and soon the carcass is laid upon the flames.

"Why have you sacrificed this animal?" you whisper.

Gideon's smile is gentle. "This is a burnt offering, my son—it symbolizes our complete surrender to God. The Lord has commanded me to do this, and by obeying Him we show our dedication. Now," he continues, "we must flee. The Baal-worshipers will soon be here for their morning rituals, and they will *not* be pleased to find their altar torn down and their Asherah pole used for kindling!"

With a grin, Gideon sprints away. You race after him, as the first rays of sun paint the hillside in brilliant colors. Birds twitter sleepily, and you drink in great lungfuls of fresh, sweet air. A stone house squats on the hillside and Gideon vaults over a low wall at the back, disappearing from sight. Unsure of what you should do next, you sit in the shadows outside the house watching the rolling hillside spring into life in the light of the rising sun.

You squint into the distance as a movement attracts your attention. A group of men hurries from the direction of Baal's former altar, heading straight toward Gideon's home. An angry buzz reaches your ears even at this distance and you draw back farther into the shadows at the side of the house to watch what will happen next.

At last the group reaches the house. Their faces are an odd mixture of murderous anger and terror. "Joash!" bellows one, pounding on the wooden door with both fists. "Bring out your son, that he may die!"

"He has torn down the altar of Baal!" roars another.

A third man steps forward, his face contorted with rage. "And he has cut down the Asherah pole that was beside it! Bring out your son, Joash—he must die for this!"

The crowd falls back as the door creaks open. An older man steps out into the sunshine and you look curiously at this older version of Gideon.

Joash's eyes blaze and he squares his shoulders defiantly as he confronts the group. "Will you contend for Baal, or will you deliver him?" he thunders. "Whoever will plead for him shall be put to death by morning."

Gasps erupt from the men and their faces drain of color. Joash's lips thin into a contemptuous smile. "If Baal is a god, let him contend for himself because someone has torn down his altar!"

"Look!" quavers one of the men as Gideon steps out from the door. "He is *unharmed*—Baal did not strike him!"

An older man detaches himself from the group, his head bowed in shame. "We should have *known* better than to join in the worship of an idol," he murmurs. "Remember the prophet who went from village to village, rebuking us for fearing the gods of the Amorites, rather than remembering the one true God?"

"You are right," says another. "That is the reason for our misfortune—God has delivered us into the hands of our enemies because we have rebelled and worshiped idols."

You watch the anger on their faces dissolve into

shame as the flames of the chariot of fire dance around you. At last, you see them no more.

"The men are right," chimes the voice gently. "Israel saw the reason for their oppression and repented—and God chose Gideon to deliver them. Now you must decide between two paths. You may see Gideon's army gather at Harod Spring or you may see Gideon's army attack their oppressors."

A thrill of excitement stiffens your spine and makes your fingers tremble as you pick up the reins. Making your decision, you pull them taut.

If you decide to see Gideon gather his army, go to page 103.

If you decide to see Gideon's army attack, go to page 107.

(You Have Decided
to See Gideon Seek a Sign)

You are standing on dew-drenched ground in the still air just before dawn. A low stone house nestles on the hillside before you, and the clear crow of a cock heralds the approach of day. As you look around at the gentle hills surrounding you, everything seems to be painted in varying shades of grey; only a faint line of pink divides the sky from the hills in the distance. You move your chilly feet, and discover that they are completely soaked with dew. As the first golden beams of sun race from the horizon, the dew sparkles like thousands of prisms everywhere you look.

The door to the house creaks open, and a sleepy Gideon steps out into the dawn. After a massive yawn and stretch, he heads toward the stone winepress. Vaulting easily over the wall, Gideon stoops and retrieves something from the stone floor of the press—then stiffens in shock. You hurry toward him, your feet leaving clear imprints in the heavy dew.

"Praise be to the Lord most high!" whispers Gideon as he looks at a fluffy mass in his hands.

You peer curiously at the fleecy, irregular object—which closely resembles the lining of your own winter jacket. *It looks dry!* you think absently, wondering how it could be dry in the midst of all this dew.

Gideon beckons you urgently. "Come here!" he commands. "Look at this!"

You vault easily over the stone wall of the wine-press, and then scramble for your footing as you slip on the wet stone floor.

"The fleece is completely dry!" Gideon whispers, thrusting the wool toward you. "This is the sign!"

You frown in bewilderment. "The fleece is a sign?"

Gideon nods. "You see," he begins, looking a little embarrassed, "the Lord told me that He would deliver Israel through me. So I called for Israelites from Manasseh, Asher, Zebulun, Naphtali—and even the Abiezrites—to assemble, in order that we could attack our oppressors, the Midianites and the Amalekites." He pauses, looking off dreamily into the distance.

"And did they assemble?" you question.

"Oh, yes—but then I saw our enemy!" Gideon replies with a shudder. "Their tents stretched as far as I could see in the valley of Jezreel—and I wondered if I had misunderstood the word of the Lord," he finishes humbly. "I am just Gideon—the youngest in my father's house, and my family is the least in Manasseh. So I asked the Lord God to give me a sign that He would deliver Israel through me."

Together you climb over the stone wall of the winepress. Gideon's gaze is faraway as he continues, "I put a fleece of wool on the threshing floor. I told the Lord that on the next morning, if the fleece were wet and the ground were dry, then I would know that He would deliver Israel through me."

"What happened?" you ask, glancing at the dry fleece.

"I squeezed the fleece the next morning and was able to wring a full bowl of water from it!" he replies softly. "Yet the whole floor of the winepress was completely dry! But I was afraid that it was only chance—after all, if there had been a little dew, the rock would certainly dry before the fleece would. *So,*" Gideon continues, after taking a deep breath, "I asked for another sign. This time I asked that the ground be wet, and the fleece dry—that way I could know without doubt that the outcome would not be by chance!"

Gooseflesh ripples down your arms as you look at the sodden ground and the bone-dry fleece. Gideon's back straightens as he absently clutches the fleece to his chest. "Now we will do battle with our enemies!" he cries as he strides toward the house.

The sparkling morning disappears in the flames of your chariot. "Here is your choice," says the steed. "You may see Gideon's army gather at Harod Spring, or you may watch Gideon's army attack their enemies."

A thrill of excitement surges through you making your fingers shake with anticipation. Quickly deciding, you pull the reins taut.

If you decide to see Gideon gather his army, go to page 103.

If you decide to see Gideon's army attack, go to page 107.

(You Have Decided to See
Gideon Gather His Army)

You are standing in a little cup-like valley—a shallow depression amid surrounding hills. Thousands of men cover the hills, and their distinctive tribal patterns are bright splashes of color against the green. At your feet is a bubbling pool, its surface trembling and dancing as a trickle of a stream rushes away to tumble down the side of the nearest hill. Gideon stands, feet apart, on the other side of the pool. Calmly, he surveys the thousands who surround him.

Cupping his hands around his mouth, Gideon calls, "Whoever is afraid and trembling, let him return and depart from Mount Gilead." His voice carries easily, borne by the wind.

You watch in horror as hundreds of the men turn away, embarrassment and relief struggling in their faces. An old man beside you gasps.

"Look!" he wails in protest, pointing to a great river of Israelites hurrying away from the assembly. "Gideon—you are mad! Why did you say that?"

Gideon smiles at the old man. "Do not worry, Purah. The Lord told me that I must say that, for there are too many of us."

"TOO MANY?" Purah shrieks. "The Midianites and Amalekites and all the sons of the east cover the valley like locusts; their camels are as numerous as the sands of the seashore! *How can you say our number is too many?*"

Gideon chuckles. "When the Lord delivers the

Midianites into our hands, it must be obvious to everyone that *He* has done it. If our army is large, we may be tempted to boast that *we* have done it ourselves."

Purah shakes his head. "Two-thirds of our people have left, Gideon. It looks to me as though only about ten thousand have remained. *I* say that the Lord helps those who help themselves!"

You watch Gideon curiously as his face becomes suddenly very still and attentive—*almost as if he is listening to someone!* you decide. He pales, and panic gleams briefly in his eyes. He raises his hands to cup them around his mouth once more.

"Come here and drink—all of you!" he roars.

Purah's jaw drops in astonishment. "My master has taken leave of his senses!" he mutters. The old servant bends over the pool, hastily bringing the water to his mouth with a cupped hand. He backs away, and sits heavily on a boulder at the side of the spring.

Gideon watches carefully as young men and old come to the bubbling spring to drink. Most fling themselves flat on the ground, lapping the water thirstily—their faces dripping with water as they rise. Intrigued, you watch as only about three men in a hundred take swift drinks as Purah has done, kneeling to drink from cupped hands. At last, it seems that each man has had his fill—and the assembly watches Gideon.

Gideon takes a deep breath, and surveys his army. "Hear me!" he shouts, his voice tense. "Those of you who knelt to drink will stay with me—and all the rest of you return to your tent!"

A buzz of excitement ripples through the crowd. "What did you say, Gideon?" shouts one burly man. "Did you say that those who lapped the water as a dog laps must return to their tents?"

His face set and pale, Gideon cups his hands around his mouth. "Those who lapped the water like a dog are to return to their tents!" he roars. "Those who knelt to drink from cupped hands will stay with me!"

"Gideon—think!" protests Purah, tugging urgently on his master's arm. "These men who remained are about ten thousand in number—and none of them are afraid. They are here to do battle with our enemy because they want to—they are ready to die, if need be. If you keep only those of us who knelt to drink, you will have only about three hundred men to take into battle! *Three hundred men*, Gideon, against more than one hundred thousand of our enemy!"

Stubbornly, Gideon shakes his head. "The Lord has told me that He will deliver us, Purah. It was He who told me to separate the men in this way. How can I do anything but obey Him?"

You watch as thousands of men stream away, shaking their heads in bewilderment. The flames of the chariot surround you, and Gideon disappears from sight—but not before you hear Purah argue angrily, "But, Gideon . . . ."

"I take you now to see Gideon's army attack their oppressors," says the voice softly.

Go to page 107.

(You Have Come
to See Gideon's Army Attack)

The black night smothers you like a blanket; no moon can be seen in the inky sky. But across the invisible plains, hundreds of thousands of campfires flicker and glow in front of what must be hundreds of thousands of tents. As far as you can see, tongues of fire declare the size of the camp. You hear the noise of camels jostling each other and groaning as they settle in for the night, and you hear a softer whisper of thousands of unseen men conversing quietly as they prepare for sleep. You crouch behind a low shrub and peer anxiously into the night.

Your heart thuds violently against your ribs as an unexpected voice breaks the silence. "I am here to relieve you, soldier!" rasps a turbaned Midianite.

Another figure glides out of the shadows within reach of your hand, his metal spear point gleaming in the light of the nearest campfire. He rolls his eyes nervously toward the hills at your back.

"What is troubling you?" growls the Midianite. "Do you fear that the Israelites will surprise us this night?"

"No," the younger man says, shaking his head. "They would never be able to get past our animals without our knowing they were here."

"What is it then?" snaps the older man. "Afraid of the dark?" he grins.

The young soldier's lips compress into a thin line of irritation. "I had a vision," he snarls defensively.

The turbaned Midianite's grin fades as he watches his companion. "A loaf of barley bread was tumbling into the camp of Midian, and it came to the tent and struck it so that it fell, and turned it upside down so that the tent lay flat!"

A sharp hiss of indrawn breath makes your skin crawl, as the older soldier regards the younger in horror. "*Barley*, you say! This is nothing less than the sword of Gideon, the son of Joash, a man of Israel," he groans. "God has given Midian and all the camp into his hand!"

Your heart leaps even further into your throat as a strong hand suddenly comes from behind and clamps firmly over your mouth, pulling you roughly backwards. A low voice breathes into your ear, "Make no sound—you are safe, youngster."

You nod hastily, recognizing Gideon. He releases you, and you follow him carefully up the hill—picking your way silently. At his side, another shadowy figure climbs the hill; you scarcely breathe until the three of you have slithered over the crest.

"Master!" exclaims the man. "Did you hear that?"

Gideon's face is wreathed in smiles. "Yes, Purah, my good and faithful servant, I heard!"

The old servant's eyes are round with wonder. "There are over one hundred thousand soldiers down there—and the Lord God guided us in safety to the very place where you would overhear the dream! Just think, Gideon!" Purah almost shouts in his enthusiasm, "God planted a dream of what He would do in the mind of one soldier—and gave its interpretation to another! That's incredible—oh!"

the old man's words stumble to a halt. "You had already thought of that! *That's* why you bowed down to worship right there outside the camp!"

Gideon's arm encircles Purah affectionately. "Come, old friend—our army awaits us."

You jog behind them a short distance, and see a group of about three hundred men waiting, their eyes riveted upon Gideon's face. "Arise!" he calls triumphantly. "For the Lord has given the camp of Midian into your hands."

Swiftly, Gideon barks instructions, dividing the men into three sections. Diving into an enormous skin bag, he hastily withdraws a curly ram's horn and places it into the hand of the nearest soldier. Gideon reaches into another bag and removes a clay pitcher—while the men stare at him in puzzlement.

As he continues to hand out the horn trumpets and pitchers, Gideon swiftly gives instructions. "Light your torch and hide it beneath the pitcher— hold it in your left hand. In your right hand, hold the trumpet. Look at me, and do what I do!" he commands.

In a short while, each bewildered Israelite is equipped with a lighted torch obscured inside a clay pitcher, as well as with a ram's horn trumpet. *How are they going to hold a weapon?* you worry. You watch Purah practically dance with excitement as at last the group—led by Gideon—creeps down the mountain toward the sleeping Midianites below. Silently, the Israelites melt into the shadows at the outskirts of the camp. *They're going to surround the camp!* you decide, astonished. *How can they ever win this way, outnumbered roughly four hundred forty Midianites to one unarmed Israelite?*

You watch as Gideon and his companions raise their horns to their lips. To a man, they draw a huge breath—then the haunting blast of the shofar overtakes the night. In the dark, the blast echos from the surrounding hills and becomes a deafening roar as each man sounds the call to battle. The smash of Gideon's pitcher on the ground is duplicated by three hundred men and the flaming torches spring into life. "A sword for the Lord and for Gideon!" reverberates from the mountaintops.

Midianites shriek in terror as they stumble out of their tents, flailing wildly with their swords. You gasp in astonishment as you see the enemy soldiers hack furiously at each other—the camp is in total confusion! Robes swirl as Midianites leap on camel back, fleeing on the swift Arabian animals into the night. Those who do not run for their lives are killing each other off at a furious rate.

Leaping flames engulf you, and you are back in the chariot of fire once more—your heart thudding with excitement.

"What happened?" your words tumble out. "Did Gideon's army win?"

The steed's bell-like laughter chimes, "Oh yes, little one—the Lord did indeed deliver Israel through Gideon."

"But they never even used weapons!" you gasp, knowing that you will never forget the miracle you have witnessed this night.

"What need had they of weapons when the Lord fought their battle?" says the steed softly. "Your

quest is almost finished now, little one. Here is your final choice. You may go back in time to see Moses appoint the first judges over Israel—or you may go forward in time to hear the prophet Hosea warn what will happen to Israel when she rebels, and worships idols."

Confused, you wonder which would be the best choice. Perhaps you could learn exactly *what* a judge is from Moses—but on the other hand, you are learning that Israel doesn't fare well as a nation when she forgets God. Uncertain, you pull the reins taut as you make your decision.

If you decide to go back in time to Moses, go to page 15.

If you decide to go forward in time to Hosea, go to page 142.

(You Have Come to See
Jephthah the Judge)

The cheerful crackle of a campfire blends with the soothing sound of crickets as you find yourself facing a broad-shouldered man across the dancing fire. His arms are scarred, his muscles sinewy, and his eyes are deep wells of quiet. An older man, his curly hair peppered with grey, is resting on a log, stretching out his hands to warm them by the fire.

"Well, Jephthah!" the older man begins, "Do you trust the elders of Gilead?"

"They have appointed me captain," Jephthah replies quietly.

The older man snorts in contempt. "Ha! That is only because they have no other warrior like you to lead them against the Ammonites! How can you forget that your own half brothers — sons of Gilead — threw you out in the cold? You are a son of Gilead too, and you had a right to your father's home even if your mother *was* a harlot!" he finishes with a furious scowl.

Jephthah's smile is crooked as he murmurs, "I must not hold their sins against them, Michael. All of Israel has cried out to the Lord in repentance — they have put away their foreign gods. My half brothers are sorry, and I cannot hold a grudge against them when I am needed to fight against the Ammonites."

Michael rises slowly, clapping Jephthah on the back in gruff affection. "Well," he grumbles, "there is no one in a battle I'd trust with my life more than you! You will be a good judge over Israel!".

Jephthah notices you and smiles kindly. "I have a daughter," he says, "who looks at me in just that way when she is bursting with questions."

You take a deep breath. "Why does God appoint judges?" you question.

Jephthah leans forward, his hands palm downward on his knees. "The answer to that question is simple, my friend. Sometimes, when people have no leader to remind them of the way they must go, they lose their way. So it has been with the children of Israel," he says with a weary sigh. "Moses was a strong leader, and although he had terrible trouble with a rebellious people, no one was ever in doubt of what was right or wrong. Moses appointed Joshua, who was also a strong leader—but after Joshua's death, a generation arose who did not know the Lord, or the mighty works He did for Israel."

Jephthah pauses, his gaze distant. At last he continues. "And the people of Israel sinned greatly, and worshiped Baal and Ashtoreth—they even took heathen spouses and failed to teach their children anything about the Lord God."

"Is that why the Lord allowed the nations around Israel to oppress her?" you ask breathlessly.

Unshed tears sparkle in Jephthah's eyes, and he nods. "Absolutely!" he replies. "And under the yoke of oppression, the people remembered God and cried out to Him for deliverance."

"But . . . " you stammer, "wasn't the punishment awfully harsh?"

Jephthah's thick brows meet in a frown. "*Harsh?*" he exclaims. "What good would it do Israel to live soft lives and forget the *Creator*? The Lord God told father Abraham that in him *all the earth would be blessed*—how will that ever happen if no one in all the earth remembers His holy name?! Listen, little one," Jephthah speaks in earnest as he leans forward, placing his scarred hands on your shoulders. "We must pray that the Lord will always raise up those who will lead His people back to Him—for in Him is all truth. Without God, people will only stumble blindly through this life—no better than the beasts of the field. I do not think," he finishes softly, "that He created us for that purpose."

The dancing flames engulf you, and the judge Jephthah disappears. Reluctantly you take the reins, knowing that this adventure is over. As the flames whirl about you, depositing you back in the twentieth century, you think about what you have seen. How many times did God give His people the opportunity to repent and obey Him again? How many men—and women—did God send to warn the Israelites of what was sure to happen? How many marvelous, awesome miracles did God perform to show His people His mighty power? You sigh and shake your head, wondering why God's children never seem to get the message. But, the memories of the steed's gentle admonitions remind you that *your* job is to judge yourself! Picking yourself up off the ground and dusting off your twentieth-century clothes, you resolve never to forget what you have learned on this journey.

THE END

(You Have Decided
to See the Philistines)

Fluffy white clouds drift lazily across a deep-blue sky. Golden fields of grain spill down gentle slopes toward thick groves of trees. Across the narrow valley below, you see the same pattern of trees, with more fields marching up the slope opposite. Turning to look uphill, you see a walled city. Outside the city gates an excited buzz of activity reaches your ears—and you head quickly toward the sound. As you reach the crest of the hill, you see the source of the noise: merchants are clustered outside the tall gates and the daily business of shopping is in full swing.

Tall Philistine soldiers saunter arrogantly through the crowds, inspecting whatever catches their eyes. Sunshine flashes off their distinctive helmets, which appear to be vertical plumes of feathers set into decorated metal headbands. Clean-shaven and bare-chested, the Philistine soldiers don't look very menacing here, you decide.

As you draw closer to the marketplace, you see a procession of Israelites hurrying toward the city, huge baskets of fruit and grain balanced easily on their heads. *Are they bringing tribute?* you wonder uneasily. You watch as the Israelites set their produce down in the market place, obviously at ease. A Philistine soldier wanders up to a Hebrew man and speaks softly. Suddenly both of them laugh uproariously, clapping each other on the back while they share the joke. *The Philistine and the Hebrew are friends with each other*! you think in surprise. You make your way slowly through the chattering crowds, past baskets of fruit, vividly painted pottery, bleating goats, and the total confusion of almost everyone talking at once. Passing through the huge bronze gates, you enter the Philistine town itself.

A friendly hand taps you on the shoulder. "Good morning, young stranger!"

An Israelite man leading a calf on a tether smiles invitingly. "You have the look of a newcomer to this city."

Nodding, you wonder why you have an uneasy feeling about this man. He seems so friendly, and yet . . . there is just something about him that you do *not* like!

"Ah!" he breathes. "Then come with me. No newcomer should miss seeing the beautiful temple of Dagon!"

The man propels you insistently toward a massive stone building just ahead. He pushes you unwillingly past a soldier standing guard impassively before a small antechamber. Passing through the dim room, you blink as the incense-laden air of the temple proper stings your eyes. Tall columns ending in lotus blossom shapes soar fifteen or twenty feet to the ceiling. Two rows of these columns end before a table on which incense is smoldering. In the shadows at the far end of the room you see a huge stone statue. The Israelite follows your glance, and smiles approvingly.

"You see the great god Dagon!" he whispers. "I sacrifice every year to him to insure that my harvest is bountiful—and it always is!"

Gooseflesh crawls up your arms as you look at the monstrous pagan statue of a bearded and crowned man, whose torso ends in the tail of a fish. Before you can stop yourself, you protest in outrage, "But you're an Israelite, aren't you? How can you sacrifice to an idol?"

The friendly smile vanishes, to be replaced by an anger so fierce that you back away. "Yes, I'm an Israelite!" He fairly spits out the words. "But I sacrifice to whom I wish! Dagon is the god of grain—and my Philistine wife taught me about him. What joy is there for a man in following the God of Abraham—do this, don't do that! In the temples of Dagon and Ashtoreth and Baalzebub, a man may have much pleasure!"

You back away in horror. "You mean this is your choice? Aren't the Philistines oppressing your people?"

"Oppression—bah!" he sneers. "So they rule over us. What of it? We trade with them, and they with us—where is the oppression? I don't care who rules over me as long as I get a good price for my grain!"

Deliberately, the man turns his back on you. Relieved, you stumble out of the temple, feeling filthy and defiled. You almost shout with relief when the flames of the chariot engulf you.

"There are many different kinds of oppression, little one," says the steed softly. "The Israelite you have just seen was indeed oppressed, though he does not recognize it. He has been overwhelmed by the gods of the Philistines, and has not stood against them as he should.

"Now it is time for another decision. You may see Samson's parents, just after the angel announces his birth to them."

"An *angel* announces Samson's birth?" you question in amazement.

Splintering chimes of laughter sparkle in the silence. "Yes, my friend. Or, you may go to Samson's home after he has chosen a wife. Which time would you rather visit?"

You have no idea which might be more helpful, so you make your decision quickly.

If you decide to see Samson's parents, go to page 123.

If you decide to go to Samson's home, go to page 126.

(You Have Decided to See Samson's Parents)

You find yourself in a golden field of grain. All around you the breeze makes a soft shushing noise by rippling the stalks of grain. You recognize the city on the hills opposite you—it is the same Philistine city you have just left. Here and there across the ripe fields people are harvesting the grain. Your attention is suddenly attracted by a woman who rushes frantically across the field toward gnarled olive trees not far away.

"Manoah! Husband!" she sobs.

Shading his eyes with a forearm, a tall man straightens from his work in the field. "Here I am!" he calls.

You wade through the sea of grain toward him as his wife flings herself into the man's outstretched arms. He looks down at her in concern as she clings to him, laughing and sobbing.

"A man of God came to me!" she gasps, between sobs.

"Now, now . . . " the man says softly, a worried frown creasing his forehead.

"And his appearance was like the appearance of an angel of God—very awesome! And I did not ask him where he came from, nor did he tell me his name."

Manoah's incredulous gaze is locked on his wife's earnest face. Placing his hands on her shoulders, he holds her slightly away from him—his eyes are wide with astonishment.

The woman grows calmer under her husband's steady gaze, and she continues more slowly, "He said to me, 'Behold, you shall conceive and give birth to a son.'"

A look of wild hope springs into Manoah's eyes. "A son!" he cries. "We had given up all hope of having a child!"

The woman nods happily. "It is true, my dear! We shall have a son. But listen to what else the man of God told me. He said that I must not drink wine or strong drink, nor eat any unclean thing—for the boy shall be a Nazirite to God from the womb to the day of his death, and he shall begin to deliver Israel from the hands of the Philistines!"

Manoah nods, a slow smile of joy lighting his face. "A son," he murmurs. "But if he is to be a Nazirite—holy to the Lord—we must know what to do with the boy." He raises his face skyward. "0 Lord, please let the messenger whom Thou has sent come to us again, that he may teach us what to do for the boy who is to be born."

Radiant flames surround you and the musical voice of the steed sounds softly in your ears. "Do you know what a Nazirite is, little one?"

"No," you answer simply.

"Nazirite means separated, or consecrated. A person who takes this vow lives a simple life which is wholly dedicated to God."

You remember that Samson's strength had something to do with his hair and ask in bewilderment, "Did Samson's strength come from his long hair?"

The silvery sound of chimes surrounds you, and you realize that the steed is laughing. "No, little one, Samson's hair did not give him strength. But a Nazirite's long hair was a symbol to those around him that he had taken the Nazirite's vows, one of which was never to cut his hair. Uncut hair was an *outward* sign of an *inner* fellowship with God. Because Samson life was dedicated to God, He endowed Samson with strength far surpassing any man's so that Samson, in turn, could use that mighty strength for the Lord. All who looked at this miracle of strength knew that it came from the Lord.

"Now you shall see Samson's parents once again," says the voice softly. "I will take you forward in time, where you will see Samson as a young man."

Great! you think happily, as you pick up the reins and wait.

Go to page 126.

(You Have Decided
to Go to Samson's Home)

Sunlight splashes against the rough walls of a small courtyard where a woman sits cross-legged on the ground, turning a mill stone. She looks up at you with a smile, inviting you to come nearer.

"Good morning, young stranger!" she says. "You must be here to help my husband with the sheep shearing. He will be back in a few moments." Uncertain what to say, you keep silent.

Just then, a tall man hustles into the courtyard, his honest face beaming. "My dear," he calls out happily, "I have just heard that Samson is on his way home!"

The woman stops turning the mill stone and claps her hands as a delighted trill of laughter escapes her. "Manoah! Then we may be a family again!"

The man chuckles. "I wonder what marvelous things our son found in the city of Timnah!" Just then a young man bursts through the low arched doorway. *This is Samson!* you think in awe. Samson's dark hair hangs in seven thick braids. His face is flushed and excited as he hugs first his father, and then his mother. You look intently at this well-built, handsome young man with a confident—perhaps just a bit arrogant—attitude.

"I saw a woman in Timnah . . . ." says Samson, suppressed excitement in every line of his body.

Manoah throws his head back, laughing heartily. "I am sure you did, my son."

Samson frowns a little, setting his jaw mutinously. "She is one of the daughters of the Philistines; get her for me as a wife."

Samson's mother stares at her son, her expression troubled. Manoah's face drains of color. "Samson, Samson. Is there no woman among the daughters of your own tribe of Dan, or among all our people, that you go to take a wife from the Philistines?" he pleads.

"Get her for me," demands Samson, his brow like a thundercloud, "for she is right in my eyes." Samson storms through the courtyard and up the steps. His father and mother seem totally unaware of your presence as they stare after him.

Manoah shakes his head. "We have no choice but to do as he asks," he moans. "But Samson's choice of wife cannot be the Lord's choice!"

"But Samson is a Nazirite!" protests his mother. "Set apart to the Lord from before his birth! How can he wish to marry a *Philistine*—a worshiper of vile idols? What have we done wrong, Manoah?" she laments, wringing her hands.

Gently, Manoah takes his wife's hands between his own. "We must trust the Lord God to bring good from this situation, my dear. Are you forgetting that the angel of the Lord performed wonders in our very sight, before he ascended to heaven in the flame of our altar?" The woman's sobs cease, as she remembers.

The sight of the husband and wife wavers and disappears as the flames engulf you.

"How can Samson do that?" you whisper, thinking of his parents' anguish.

"Have you never known *anyone* to ignore the advice of his parents? Furthermore, you may be forgetting that Samson was reared from birth to be a servant of the Lord. Do you not think it possible that the Lord God is now beginning to put His plan into action by allowing Samson to become involved with the Philistines?"

Humbled, you decide that you had better leave the judging of Samson's life up to the One who is responsible for judging!

"Now here is your decision," chimes the voice more gently. "You may go some twenty years into the future and see some changes that have occurred in Israel because of Samson's leading. His wife is now dead and Samson has taken up with a harlot named Delilah. You may see Samson and Delilah, or you may see Samson after his capture by the Philistines. Which will you choose?"

Wow! you think, *How could Samson ever choose to be with a harlot? What happened to his dedication to God?* But the memory of what just happened when you dared to judge Samson's behavior is still ringing in your ears, so you decide to say nothing. *How will either choice help me on my quest?* you wonder in bewilderment. Hastily you decide, then pull the reins taut.

If you decide to see Samson and Delilah, go to page 130.

If you decide to see Samson after his capture, go to page 135.

(You Have Decided to See Samson and Delilah)

Your back presses against a wide wooden balustrade overlooking a spacious courtyard. A knot of richly-robed men crowds between you and the arched doorway of a second-story room, where a young woman stands. Her full, painted lips pout as she surveys the men.

"Well?" she purrs. "Have you brought the money? Samson has told me all that is in his heart—I know the secret of his great strength."

"All eleven hundred pieces of silver, Delilah!" answers one of the men. He steps forward, handing the woman a large cloth bag. "What a temptress you are!" he adds with a leer.

Delilah snatches the bag greedily, her eyes sparkling. She is exquisitely beautiful, but her eyes are cold—you shiver as you look at the face of betrayal. "Three times Samson deceived me about the source of his strength—but not this time!" she snaps. "I will show you where to hide—and when the mighty Samson has been robbed of his strength, he is all yours!"

You jump as the man in front turns to you suddenly. "So you wish to see the fall of Samson?" he sneers. "Very well—you may wait and watch with us!" He propels you forward with the group into a small room. A richly-embroidered curtain hangs over the door to the connecting room. Miserably, you press against the wall and wait. A low murmur of voices issues from the next room, and you think you recognize Samson's voice. The Philistine men are tense with anticipation, murderous revenge is stamped upon every face. After what seems an eternity, a voice growls low in your ear.

"Look into the room, dog!" hisses the Philistine. "But *carefully*—we do not wish Samson to know we are here!" He pushes you toward the curtain and you quietly pull it back an infinitesimal bit to look into the room.

An oil lamp paints dancing shadows on the walls of the small room. Delilah lounges triumphantly amidst piles of brightly-colored cushions, and a sleeping Samson lies with his head in her lap. Bent over Samson is a huge man, holding a razor poised above Samson's head. You drop the curtain back into place as a painful pinch on your arm recalls you to your Philistine companions.

"Well?" the man mouths. Pushing you roughly aside, he moves the curtain himself, then grins over his shoulder at the other men. "She is having him shaved! He will soon be ours!"

Sick at heart—for you know that Samson should *never* have revealed that the secret of his strength was in his Nazirite vow, of which uncut hair was the sign—you move slowly away from the group of men. A burly arm shoots out, stopping your progress.

"Oh no you don't!" hisses your captor, grinning wickedly. "You shall see what we Philistines do to our enemies!"

Rage washes over you. "But Samson has only been judging the Israelites," you explode. "What's he ever done to you?"

His eyes narrow as a flush of rage mounts on his face. Hatred sparkles in his dark eyes as he growls, "What has he done? Samson has killed more than a thousand Philistines, besides burning our fields, vineyards, and olive groves! Once, we gathered at the gates of Gaza to capture him when he left in the morning. While we waited for him we slept, and as we were sleeping, Samson *lifted* the gate and gate posts from the ground and carried them—bar and all—to the top of the hill behind us!"

You start to snicker at the image of this band of would-be tough guys waking up to find a gaping hole in the city wall—but you look into the murderous eyes of the one who has been speaking and decide against it.

"He made us look like fools!" the man spits out. "For all these things he will die! But first," he adds with an evil smile, "we will humble the mighty Samson—that will be entertainment indeed!"

Suddenly Delilah's voice rings out gleefully from behind the curtain. "The Philistines are upon you, Samson!"

The Philistines spring into the room, ripping down the curtain in their haste. Through the door you see Samson leap to his feet and you gasp at the sight of his hastily-shorn hair. Danger sparks from his eyes, and the Philistines pause for a moment— then seize hold of Samson. With a roar of rage, Samson lunges to free himself; the Philistines grit their teeth and hang on. With a mighty shudder Samson struggles to fling off his captors—and you see in his face the realization that the Lord has departed from him—and with His departure, the

superhuman strength is gone. Terrible anguish and grief twist Samson's features as you watch in helpless horror.

A Philistine man faces Samson, his back rigid with hatred. He spits full in the Israelite's face—and fast as thought—gouges out Samson's eyes. Delilah shrieks in delight, and you stumble away from the door, retching in grief and revulsion. Sinking to your knees, you do not even notice that you are once again in the chariot until the gentle voice speaks.

"Be comforted, little one," says the steed softly. "Samson will turn again to the Lord."

"But why?" you cry in anguish. "Why did God take away Samson's strength?"

You feel breathless in the heavy silence that follows, but you cannot help asking, "Why would the Lord leave Samson in the hands of his enemies?"

Infinitely patient, the voice chimes. "Do you not see the true sorrow? *Samson did not even notice that the Spirit of the Lord had left him*! Only when his strength was gone did he know that the Lord was gone. That is the grief that Samson must bear—he was blessed with the Lord's Spirit from his mother's womb, yet the charms of a woman meant more to him than the Lord. Of his own choice, Samson violated his promise to God; and the Lord God has given us all the power to choose."

"It is time for you to see Samson in captivity," says the steed gently. Full of sorrow, you pick up the reins.

Go to page 135.

(You Have Come to
See Samson In Captivity)

A huge crowd of people surrounds you and a festive feeling is in the air. Gaily-embroidered, ankle-length tunics seem to be the order of the day, and the odor of beer assails your nostrils. Standing on tip-toe, you peer between shoulders down a narrow corridor lined on both sides with richly-decorated pillars. The smoke of burning incense billows from an altar at the end of the corridor and stings your eyes. A niche in the wall behind the incense table holds a statue of a crowned man, his torso ending in a fish tail. Mounds of grain and fruit are everywhere and you decide this must be a religious celebration of some kind.

A raucous voice floats down from above. "Bring Samson to us, so that he may amuse us!"

You look up and see that deep balconies, jammed with merry-makers, completely surround the pillared hall. Almost every face is flushed—either with drink or excitement.

A man beside you guffaws loudly. "Our god has given our enemy Samson into our hands—even the destroyer of our country, who has slain many of us!"

"Samson! Bring us the blind hero!" someone shrieks. "Let the blind man entertain us!"

The crowd suddenly grows quiet, and you feel waves of hatred hit you like a physical blow. All attention is directed to a spot behind you and you twist around to look. What you see makes you sick at heart—Samson, led by a young boy, walks haltingly into the temple of Dagon. The empty sockets where his eyes used to be are dark holes in a face lined with pain and sorrow. His neck is raw and bleeding under the metal collar, and he is filthy from prison.

"Hey! Strong man!" sneers a voice in the crowd. "Our god Dagon has delivered you into our hands—where is *your* God?"

Samson whirls around at the sound of the voice, fury in his sightless face.

"Bow your knee to Dagon, Israelite dog!" calls another voice. The crowd roars with laughter as Samson turns this way and that with each shouted insult, struggling vainly to face his enemy. Soon mocking calls fill the air and the crowd's hatred rises to a fever pitch.

You work your way through the crowd to get closer to Samson, studying his face—for there is some new emotion on his tortured face. A thrill of excitement races like fire in your veins as you realize that Samson's hair has begun to grow again!

He bends over the boy holding his hand and murmurs, "Let me feel the pillars on which the house rests, that I may lean against them."

The boy snickers as he leads Samson toward the very center of the columned hall. He places Samson's right hand upon one pillar and his left upon another—then aims a vicious kick at the blind man's shin. You see pain on Samson's face, but instead of anger, his expression melts into one of measureless peace as he raises his face heavenward.

"O Lord God," his voice throbs with emotion,

"please remember me and please strengthen me this one, last time. O God, give me Thy strength, that I may be avenged of the Philistines for my two eyes!" He moves his hands on the columns, shifting his feet until they are shoulder-width apart. Samson's frame tenses and you can almost *see* supernatural power begin to flow through his tortured body. His lips move soundlessly in prayer and a smile begins to spread across his face as a tiny cracking noise is heard.

"Look!" a shrill voice calls drunkenly. "Our enemy is trying to pull Dagon's temple down!" Waves of harsh laughter spread—so loud that no one hears the creaking noise growing louder.

The leaping flames of your chariot engulf you, but this time you can still see Samson's face through the flames—triumphant and adoring. The pillars split with a loud crack and a terrible rumble follows. Laughter turns to shrieks as the temple roof begins to crumble, pillars sway and fall, and the walls rock inward. You have one last glimpse of Samson's glowing face before the flames blot him from view.

You find that you are trembling violently, and hold on to the side of the chariot with white-knuckled hands. "He didn't ask to be freed," you breathe. "Samson was willing to die with the Philistines!"

"Yes, little one," answers the steed softly. "Samson came back to the Lord God at the end."

"But I don't understand how he got so far away from the Lord in the first place!" you complain. "How could a man *dedicated* to God get mixed up with a harlot?"

The voice of the steed chimes softly in answer. "God doesn't force anyone to do anything. In His grace and wisdom, He gives us choices and abilities. What we do with these opportunities is left to our own free will. It could be that Samson's pride caused him to forget that his strength was from the Lord, and his desire for Delilah replaced his desire to please God. Yes, little one, even a person dedicated to the Lord can, and often does, take a mighty fall."

You think for a moment about the people of your own day who try to obey God but often sin. Then several questions pop into your head. "But all the good that Samson did was not destroyed by his sin, was it?" you ask the steed. "And, in the end, he did come back to the Lord, right? Didn't Samson accomplish what he was supposed to?"

"This is more evidence of God's grace toward us and His almighty power; that He uses our lives for His purpose in spite of our weaknesses, and that He continues to love and forgive us." replies the steed. "And yes, Samson's job was to *begin* to deliver Israel, and that he did.

"But now it is time for another choice. You may go back to the very beginning of the period of the judges to see Moses appoint the first judges over Israel, or you may visit the prophet Hosea, who lived some three hundred years after the death of Samson. From Hosea, you will find out whether or not the Israelites finally learned their lesson about straying from the Lord."

Confused, you wonder which destination would be the best choice. Perhaps you could learn exactly *what* a judge is from Moses—but on the other hand, you would like to know if Israel remained faithful after the period of the judges. Uncertain, you pull the reins taut and make your decision.

If you decide to go back in time to Moses, go to page 15.

If you decide to go forward in time to Hosea, go to page 142.

(You Have Decided
to See the Prophet Hosea)

Black thunderclouds boil overhead, and lightning slices the turbulent sky. Gusts of wind tear at your tunic, and hail pommels your face. You squint into the wind to see a twisted tree clinging to a jagged hillside. Holding a forearm across your eyes for protection, you sprint toward the tree. You reach the scant protection with a sigh of relief, and huddle close to the scrawny trunk.

"You seek protection when there is none!"

Startled, you twist around to see a man slumped forlornly on a low rock on the other side of the tree. The wind howls and shrieks and you are certain that you must have misunderstood him. Blood trickles down from a cut above his eye and his tunic is soaked with rain. "Are you hurt?" you ask uncertainly.

The man's face is carved deeply with lines of pain and sorrow, but he smiles gently. "No, my friend I am not hurt—but Israel, oh Israel," he ends with a sob in his throat. "You are not a child of Israel?" he asks.

"No," you answer. "But I am a friend of Israel."

The man's face lights with kindness. "That is good, youngster. But Israel has sown the wind, and shall reap the whirlwind!"

Electrified, you stammer, "Who are you, and what do you mean, please?"

He shakes his head sorrowfully, tears streaming down his face and mingling with the rain. "I am Hosea, a spokesman for the Lord God, and by my words I mean that the children of Israel have turned away from God. They have rebelled against His law. They have set up kings—but not kings appointed by God. They have made idols of gold and silver—and now they dare to cry out to God that they know Him! Know Him? They have thrown their insults into the wind, and the Lord's judgement will soon fall upon them like a whirlwind!"

"What will happen?" you breathe.

"Israel will be taken captive," Hosea answers with dreadful simplicity. "In captivity, when they can no longer worship their idols, when they are poor and humbled—then they will have nowhere else to turn but to the Lord God. And then," he continues with devotion burning in his eyes, "God will say to Israel, 'You are My people!' and they will say, 'Thou art my God!'"

You stare unseeing into the stormy sky, while Hosea's sorrowful face dissolves in the firey flames of your chariot. Sadly, you think about how God's children turned from him in the days of the judges, too. And each time they did, they suffered oppression at the hands of their enemies.

Suddenly you realize you may have discovered part of the answer to your quest.

"Israel reaped the whirlwind over and over again each time she, as a nation, forgot the Lord God. Is *that* why God appointed judges—to lead Israel back to Him?" you ask the steed in excitement.

The chiming laughter follows the words that have tumbled out of your mouth. "You have almost completed your quest, little one," replies the voice. "You are right—in those days there was no king in Israel; every man did what was right in his own eyes. So, God sent judges to correct the people and lead them back into His care."

"But they apparently never learned their lesson," you note. "If Hosea lived three hundred years after Samson and now *he's* predicting Israel's destruction again!"

"To answer that would require another adventure," replies the steed. Now, however, I am going to take you backward in time to see Moses appoint the first judges over Israel."

Eagerly, you pick up the reins.

Go to page 15.